Managing Response to Significant Cyber Incidents

Comparing Event Life Cycles and Incident Response Across Cyber and Non-Cyber Events

QUENTIN E. HODGSON, AARON CLARK-GINSBERG,
ZACHARY HALDEMAN, ANDREW LAULAND, IAN MITCH

RAND HOMELAND SECURITY RESEARCH DIVISION

For more information on this publication, visit **www.rand.org/t/RRA1265-4**.

About RAND

The RAND Corporation is a research organization that develops solutions to public policy challenges to help make communities throughout the world safer and more secure, healthier and more prosperous. RAND is nonprofit, nonpartisan, and committed to the public interest. To learn more about RAND, visit www.rand.org.

Research Integrity

Our mission to help improve policy and decisionmaking through research and analysis is enabled through our core values of quality and objectivity and our unwavering commitment to the highest level of integrity and ethical behavior. To help ensure our research and analysis are rigorous, objective, and nonpartisan, we subject our research publications to a robust and exacting quality-assurance process; avoid both the appearance and reality of financial and other conflicts of interest through staff training, project screening, and a policy of mandatory disclosure; and pursue transparency in our research engagements through our commitment to the open publication of our research findings and recommendations, disclosure of the source of funding of published research, and policies to ensure intellectual independence. For more information, visit www.rand.org/about/research-integrity.

Published by the RAND Corporation, Santa Monica, Calif.

Library of Congress Cataloging-in-Publication Data is available for this publication.
ISBN: 978-1-9774-0936-2

Cover images: Michael Rieger/FEMA News Photo, InciWeb, Edwin L. Wriston/U.S. Army National Guard, and Department of Homeland Security

About This Report

The United States has a long history of preparing for and responding to large-scale incidents affecting public safety and homeland security, including multiple types of natural hazards and terror attacks. The United States does not have comparable depth of experience in responding to cyber incidents and has built its response planning and execution systems in part on the frameworks developed for other types of incident response. These factors prompt the concerns of whether cyber incidents—particularly those deemed significant—are of such a different character that they require a different approach, or whether there are lessons from which the United States can learn about these other incidents to improve its preparation to respond to cyber incidents.

This research was conducted using internal funding generated from operations of the RAND Homeland Security Research Division (HSRD) and managed within the HSRD Strategy, Policy & Operations Program. HSRD conducts research and analysis for the United States Homeland Security Enterprise, which includes the United States Department of Homeland Security, as well as the state, local, tribal, territorial, private sector, and international partners who contribute to homeland security policy. For more information on the Strategy, Policy & Operations Program, see www.rand.org/hsrd. For more information on this publication, visit www.rand.org/t/RRA1265-4.

Acknowledgments

We would like to acknowledge the important contributions to our thinking that informed this report, including through other work we have conducted. We thank Brodi Kotila for her contributions to developing the initial framework of analysis and her careful review and critique of several drafts of this report. Ben Boudreaux also provided helpful comments on earlier drafts, and Kristin Leuschner contributed significantly to improving the structure and readability of the report. We thank our reviewers, Paul Stockton and Donell Harvin, for their careful review and feedback. All errors remain the authors'.

Summary

The specter of a *significant cyber incident*—a cyber attack that results in widespread disruption to critical lifeline sectors or National Critical Functions (NCFs)[1] and in cascading impacts that affect national and homeland security, economic security, or public health and safety, including the possibility of injuries and deaths—has grown in recent years.[2] Recent events that reinforce this concern include the ransomware attacks against Colonial Pipeline and meat processor JBS in 2021 that affected operations;[3] the manipulation of chemical levels in a Florida water treatment plant in February 2021;[4] and the cyber attacks on Ukraine's power grid in 2015 and 2016.[5] These attacks did not lead to injury or death or to extensive economic damage, but are concerning developments that indicate the potential for more serious consequences in the future.

The U.S. government has recognized these threats and issued guidance for preparing to respond to such incidents, including the development of a National Cyber Incident Response Plan (NCIRP) in 2016 and recently announced efforts to improve public-private planning for incident

---

1 *NCFs* are defined as

> [F]unctions of government and the private sector so vital to the United States that their disruption, corruption, or dysfunction would have a debilitating effect on security, national economic security, national public health or safety, or any combination thereof (Cybersecurity and Infrastructure Security Agency [CISA], "National Critical Functions," webpage, undated-c).

2 White House, Office of the Press Secretary, "Presidential Policy Directive–United States Cyber Incident Coordination," presidential memorandum, July 26, 2016.

3 "JBS: Cyber-Attack Hits World's Largest Meat Supplier," *BBC News*, June 2, 2021; and William Turton and Kartikay Mehrotra, "Hackers Breached Colonial Pipeline Using Compromised Password," *Bloomberg*, June 4, 2021.

4 Maria Henriquez, "Hacker Breaks into Florida Water Treatment Facility, Changes Chemical Levels," *Security*, February 9, 2021.

5 Dragos, Inc., *Industrial Control System Threats*, Hanover, Md., March 1, 2018, p. 7; and Dragos, Inc., *CRASHOVERRIDE: Analysis of the Threat to Electric Grid Operations*, Washington, D.C., June 2017.

response.[6] Although the United States has yet to experience a cyber incident on the scale of significance warranting the elevated coordination envisioned in the NCIRP and other guidance, that day may soon be here—and it is not clear that the current approach to planning for cyber incident response is sufficient to meet the challenge.[7]

Unfortunately, the ability to respond to a significant cyber incident has not matched the growing policy attention and increasing severity and frequency of cyber incidents. At the federal level, response procedures for significant cyber incidents remain underdeveloped,[8] often built on the structures and processes developed for non-cyber emergency management.[9] For the (often private sector) infrastructure owners and operators of critical lifelines and NCFs, incident response planning has grown out of cyber incident response at an organizational level, in which the impacts are largely contained to business systems and not extended to operational technology. Whether these approaches are appropriate and sufficient to support an effective, coordinated response to a significant cyber incident in the future is an open question.

Our purpose in this report is to support public and private sector stakeholders working to improve response to a significant cyber incident by exploring where incident response plans for non-cyber events can inform preparation for cyber incident response—and where using non-cyber incident response plans as a template may be counterproductive or lead to an ineffective cyber incident response. We focus on these questions:

---

6 Department of Homeland Security, *National Cyber Incident Response Plan*, Washington, D.C., December 2016.

7 The White House did convene a Unified Coordination Group (UCG) to respond to the SolarWinds and Microsoft Exchange Server compromises revealed in December 2020 and March 2021, respectively, although these incidents arguably did not meet the threshold for a significant cyber incident. A UCG is one of the primary multiagency and multistakeholder coordination bodies called for in Presidential Policy Directive 41 and the NCIRP (see Maggie Miller, "White House 'Standing Down' Emergency Response Groups to SolarWinds, Microsoft Hacks," *The Hill*, April 19, 2021; and White House, Office of the Press Secretary, 2016).

8 Angus King and Mike Gallagher, *Cyberspace Solarium Commission: Final Report*, Arlington, Va., March 2020, p. 17.

9 Department of Homeland Security, 2016, pp. 6–7.

- What are the similarities and differences between cyber incidents and other incidents in terms of how they occur?
- Given these similarities and differences, how might they affect the types of decisions incident responders have to make, activities that responders need to undertake, and information available to them to inform those decisions and activities?
- Do these distinctions, in turn, call for a different approach to cyber incident response, or are the current structures, mechanisms, and approaches sufficiently adaptable to account for the distinctions?

To answer these questions, this report examines how incident response occurs for several types of incidents—terrorist incidents, natural hazards, public health emergencies, and cyber incidents—to understand key characteristics of and impacts from those incidents, how they affect incident response, and how each incident type is distinct from the others. This report examines these incidents in terms of key features of their incident life cycles—how they emerge and play out over time—and how these phases and consequent impacts affect decisionmaking in response.

Key Findings

Table S.1 summarizes some of the key characteristics of each incident type and response and how they differ from each other. The table highlights that the preparations for significant cyber incidents are more complex due to the low likelihood of advanced warning, the high degree of uncertainty around the scope and scale of an incident, the relative inexperience with responding to significant cyber incidents, and the high degree of diversity across response stakeholders. The ratings of *high*, *moderate*, or *low* are relative ratings to indicate the distinctions between the types of incidents and are not scaled to specific measures.

We note that the table is derived from an examination of a limited number of prior incidents for each type and reflects contingent analysis of how each of the incident types differ in ways that are relevant to decisionmaking in incident response. It is possible that examination of a larger number of incidents of each type could yield different characterizations.

TABLE S.1
Comparison of Incident Types

Incident Type	Warning of Incident?	Degree of Uncertainty in Early Incident Stages	Level of Responder Experience	Diversity of Responder Communities
Terrorist incidents	Sometimes	High	High	Moderate
Natural hazards	Sometimes	Moderate	High	Moderate
Public health emergencies	Sometimes	Moderate to high	Moderate to high	High
Significant cyber incidents	Rare	High	Low to moderate	High

Recommendations

Planning and preparing for a significant cyber incident response is a priority for the U.S. government. To address the challenges, we recommend several actions.

Improving Exercises to Address Critical Uncertainties in Response Planning and Execution

CISA and other government stakeholders involved in incident response planning should consider developing a series of exercises that focus on the different challenges we have identified. First, the series would examine incident identification and assessment, followed by a focus on when and how to declare a significant cyber incident and mobilize resources, and concluding with scenarios that test transition points.

Conducting Analysis to Inform Incident Identification

The first step in responding to a significant cyber incident is to know when it is occurring. Because the vectors that can lead to a *standard* cyber incident and a *significant* cyber incident are often similar, and often occur well in advance of the incident's discovery or effects manifest, differentiating between the two in the early stages is a challenge. In the circumstances in which the initial stages are not detected until it is too late, organizations would benefit from having a clearer understanding of the potential grave impacts of a cyber incident—the secondary and tertiary effects that often lead to the most significant consequences. This involves analysis of the ways in which complex systems can fail and lead to cascading effects so that cyber incident responders and other entities can establish indicators to watch out for.

Determining When a Significant Cyber Incident Has Occurred and Warrants Activating Joint Public-Private Incident Response Plans

The NCIRP states that a "Cyber UCG will be formed and activated only in the event of a significant cyber incident" and provides several mechanisms for convening the Cyber UCG, but it is unclear who ultimately makes the determination that a significant cyber incident is occurring.[10] The declaration of a significant cyber incident does not automatically trigger any particular response, and such a classification currently does not confer any additional authority, such as allowing the federal government to intervene to respond domestically. Domestic cyber incident response still largely depends on voluntary coordination and cooperation between the public and private sectors. CISA has identified this factor as an area requiring additional work, and one in which joint public-private contingency planning can help identify required information and agreed mechanisms for such a declaration.[11]

---

[10] Department of Homeland Security, 2016.

[11] The Homeland Security Operational Analysis Center (HSOAC), a federally funded research and development center operated by RAND on behalf of the Department of Homeland Security, has developed a contingency planning how-to guide, planning template, and an accompanying introductory guide for decisionmakers to support planning efforts that can further these discussions. Brodi Kotila, Quentin E. Hodgson, Benjamin Boudreaux, Ian Mitch, Aaron Clark-Ginsberg, Sale Lilly, Kristin J. Leuschner, Tom Wingfield, *Planning for Significant Cyber Incidents: An Introduction for Decisionmakers*, Homeland Security Operational Analysis Center operated by the RAND Corporation, RR-A1265-1, forthcoming.

Areas for Further Research

These recommendations are intended to further planning and learning among stakeholders to better prepare for future responses. In addition to these practical steps, we conclude that there are more areas requiring further research. To improve incident management, there is a need for continued empirical work focused on the governance structures for different significant events. This work would delve deeper into addressing who the incident responders are, the types of capabilities they bring to bear, and how those responders integrate those capabilities currently in response. Further research into how these stakeholders coordinate their efforts currently and collaborate to determine, based on real-world experience and exercises, what forms of collaboration are most effective, and where coordination can break down would vastly improve planning and execution of response.

Response to significant incidents of the types we explore here is a multistakeholder endeavor, involving collaboration across government agencies and different sectors of society. In some incidents this networked response appears to operate effectively in extreme conditions, creating a reliable response even when the structures, processes, and individual responders may not be fully prepared to respond. However, there are also many examples of failure in which effective response foundered because of unreliable, incomplete or unprepared response infrastructure, processes, or organizations. More research is needed to focus on the network, identifying the conditions that can be put in place to ensure response networked reliability. This would provide the Department of Homeland Security and other incident responders a path forward for targeting investments to ensure response to significant incident.

Contents

About This Report ... iii
Summary ... v
Figures and Tables ... xiii

CHAPTER ONE
Introduction ... 1
Purpose of This Report ... 6
Approach ... 7
Limitations ... 9
What Is Emergency Management and Incident Response? ... 9
Organization of This Report ... 14

CHAPTER TWO
Key Features of Non-Cyber Incidents ... 15
Terrorist Incidents ... 15
Natural Hazards ... 25
Public Health Emergencies ... 32

CHAPTER THREE
Life Cycle of Significant Cyber Incidents ... 41
Phases of a Significant Cyber Incident ... 43

CHAPTER FOUR
Cross-Incident Analysis ... 61
Incident Origins, Identification, and Attribution May Consume Cyber Incident Response Resources ... 61
Who Responds Differs Across Incident Types; Cyber Incident Response Will Be Led by Private Sector–Affected Entities ... 62
Decisionmaking Is Often More Complex in Cyber Incidents ... 64
Implications for Cyber Incident Response ... 66

CHAPTER FIVE
Recommendations and Areas for Future Research ... 69
Recommendations ... 69
Areas for Further Research ... 72

Abbreviations 75
References 77

Figures and Tables

Figures

3.1. Cyber Kill Chain® 45
3.2. Cyber Incident Response and Recovery Life Cycle 50
3.3. Examples of Decision Points for Cyber Incident Response 56
3.4. Potential Paths to Cyber Incident Response Failures 58

Tables

S.1. Comparison of Incident Types viii
4.1. Comparison of Incident Types 65

CHAPTER ONE

Introduction

The specter of a *significant cyber incident*—a cyber attack that results in widespread disruption to critical lifeline sectors or National Critical Functions (NCFs),[1] and cascading impacts that affect national and homeland security, economic security, or public health and safety, including the possibility of injuries and deaths—has grown in recent years.[2] Events in recent years have heightened this concern. Ransomware attacks against Colonial Pipeline and meat processor JBS in 2021 resulted in impacts to operations.[3] Unidentified hackers briefly manipulated chemical levels in a Florida water treatment plant in February 2021.[4] Since the cyber attacks on Ukraine's power grid in 2015 and 2016, the number of incidents affect critical infrastructure has increased alarmingly.[5] To date the United States has not

[1] *NCFs* are defined as

> [F]unctions of government and the private sector so vital to the United States that their disruption, corruption, or dysfunction would have a debilitating effect on security, national economic security, national public health or safety, or any combination thereof. (Cybersecurity and Infrastructure Security Agency [CISA], "National Critical Functions," webpage, undated-c)

[2] White House, Office of the Press Secretary, "Presidential Policy Directive – United States Cyber Incident Coordination," webpage, July 26, 2016.

[3] William Turton and Kartikay Mehrotra, "Hackers Breached Colonial Pipeline Using Compromised Password," *Bloomberg*, June 4, 2021; and "JBS: Cyber-Attack Hits World's Largest Meat Supplier," *BBC News*, June 2, 2021.

[4] Maria Henriquez, "Hacker Breaks into Florida Water Treatment Facility, Changes Chemical Levels," *Security*, February 9, 2021.

[5] Dragos, Inc., *Industrial Control System Threats*, Hanover, Md., March 1, 2018, p. 7; and Dragos, Inc., *CRASHOVERRIDE: Analysis of the Threat to Electric Grid Operations*, Washington, D.C., June 2017

experienced a truly large-scale cyber incident resulting in significant consequences as defined in U.S. national policy, though some events such as the 2017 NotPetya attacks that disrupted multiple sectors worldwide were widespread and costly.[6] The lack of exposure to a significant cyber incident is positive, but the United States cannot remain complacent and needs to prepare to respond to a significant cyber incident when—as many experts predict—one inevitably occurs.

As cyber threats and their potential impacts grow, particularly the potential for incidents that can have significant consequences, the need to plan for coordinated response is even greater. Numerous reports point to the growth in cyber incidents of all types, including cybercrime, and nation-state espionage.[7] In 2020 (the most recent year's reporting available at the time of writing), the Federal Bureau of Investigation (FBI) received almost 800,000 complaints (69 percent higher than 2019) to its Internet Crime Complaint Center accounting for reported losses of more than $4.1 billion.[8] The operational technology security firm Dragos identified four new threat groups targeting industrial control systems and operational technology in its 2020

---

6 Presidential Policy Directive (PPD) 41, defines a *significant cyber incident* as

> A cyber incident that is (or group of related cyber incidents that together are) likely to result in demonstrable harm to the national security interests, foreign relations, or economy of the United States or to the public confidence, civil liberties, or public health and safety of the American people (White House, Office of the Press Secretary, "Presidential Policy Directive–United States Cyber Incident Coordination," presidential memorandum, July 26, 2016).

Note that the U.S. government has convened cyber unified coordination groups (UCGs) for SolarWinds and Microsoft Exchange Server incidents, although these events arguably did not meet the threshold for a significant cyber incident. The NotPetya attacks in 2017 affected such sectors as health care and shipping and also led to losses of at least $10 billion worldwide. However, it was not declared a significant incident by the U.S. government nor did it prompt a cyber UCG to convene. See Andy Greenberg, *Sandworm: A New Era of Cyberwar and the Hunt for the Kremlin's Most Dangerous Hackers*, New York: Anchor Books, 2020, p. 199.

7 See for example, Crowdstrike, *2021 Global Threat Report*, Sunnyvale, Calif., 2021; and National Cyber Security Centre, *NCSC Annual Review 2021*, London, November 17, 2021.

8 FBI, Internet Crime Complaint Center, *Internet Crime Report 2020*, Washington, D.C., 2020.

year in review, bringing the number of groups it tracks to 15 in total.[9] This growth in the number of threat groups targeting industrial command systems and operational technology is important because it indicates greater potential for cyber incidents that can cause physical harm in addition to compromising business systems and other information technology (IT).

Successive presidential administrations in the United States starting with the Reagan administration have recognized the potential for deleterious impacts from a cyber incident and created policies, plans, and organizations to prepare for, deter, and respond to significant cyber incidents domestically and abroad.[10] The U.S. government established policy in Presidential Policy Directive (PPD) 41 and published the National Cyber Incident Response Plan (NCIRP) in December 2016, which provides the broad strategic framework for coordinating federal and other stakeholders' cyber incident response.[11] PPD-41 and the NCIRP provide the basic policy and framework for coordinating government and non-government stakeholder roles in responding to significant cyber incidents, but they do not provide detailed guidance on how each stakeholder will integrate, coordinate, or deconflict their roles in response.[12] More recently, the CISA at the Department of Homeland Security launched a joint cyber defense collaborative to develop and execute cyber defense operations plans in concert with federal interagency, private sector and state, local, territorial, and tribal (SLTT) governments and has developed planning guidance to inform NCF stakeholders' approach to planning.[13] These initiatives are useful and necessary steps

---

9 Dragos, Inc., *ICS Cybersecurity Year in Review 2020*, Washington, D.C., 2021.

10 Fred Kaplan, "'WarGames' and Cybersecurity's Debt to a Hollywood Hack," *New York Times*, February 19, 2016b.

11 Department of Homeland Security, *National Cyber Incident Response Plan*, Washington, D.C., December 2016.

12 Brodi Kotila, Quentin E. Hodgson, Benjamin Boudreaux, Ian Mitch, Aaron Clark-Ginsberg, Sale Lilly, Kristin J. Leuschner, Tom Wingfield, *Planning for Significant Cyber Incidents: An Introduction for Decisionmakers*, Homeland Security Operational Analysis Center operated by the RAND Corporation, RR-A1265-1, forthcoming, pp. 1–3.

13 CISA, "CISA Launches New Joint Cyber Defense Collaborative," webpage, August 5, 2021. The Homeland Security Operational Analysis Center (HSOAC), a federally funded research and development center operated by the RAND Corporation on behalf of the Department of Homeland Security, worked with federal partners and representatives

toward planning for significant cyber incidents, but these systems and processes remain largely untested.[14] This lack of practice means that we do not know whether existing plans, procedures, or coordination mechanisms are adequate to support response to a significant cyber incident.

Unfortunately, the ability to respond to a significant cyber incident has not matched the growing policy attention and increasing severity and frequency of cyber incidents. At the federal level, response procedures for significant cyber incidents remain underdeveloped,[15] often built on the structures and processes developed for non-cyber emergency management.[16] For the (often private sector) infrastructure owners and operators of critical lifelines and NCFs, incident response planning has grown out of cyber incident response at an organizational level, in which the impacts are largely contained to business systems and not extended to operational technology. Whether these approaches are appropriate and sufficient to support effective, coordinated response to a significant cyber incident in the future is an open question.

The NCIRP—the U.S. government's framework for cyber incident response—borrows from U.S. disaster response, emergency management, and other response planning activities (e.g., the Federal Emergency Management Agency [FEMA] provided the support structure and outreach to assist the development of the NCIRP). In some ways this gravitation toward existing structures, mechanisms, and approaches made sense because these

---

of one NCF to develop a prototype contingency plan for significant cyber incident response and subsequently developed a planning how-to guide with a planning template and a summary guide for senior decisionmakers.

14 The SolarWinds compromises discovered in late 2020 led to the White House convening a UCG with private sector participation, but this particular incident does not appear to meet the criteria for a significant cyber incident as laid out in PPD 41 (see Department of Homeland Security, 2016). The U.S. government has responded to numerous cyber incidents, but has not yet had to respond to a large-scale crisis caused by a cyber incident that truly tests public-private incident response capabilities and procedures.

15 Angus King and Mike Gallagher, *Cyberspace Solarium Commission: Final Report*, Arlington, Va., March 2020, p. 17.

16 Department of Homeland Security, 2016, pp. 6–7.

examples provided ready templates and structures to adopt that would be familiar to many in the emergency management field.

At the same time, the response plans used in other sectors may not be appropriate for cyber; moreover, response planning and execution mechanisms for non-cyber incidents have themselves fallen short at times. Although the study of emergency response is a relatively mature one,[17] we have also seen numerous examples where even seemingly well-understood events have still challenged existing response structures. This is illustrated by response challenges in connection with Hurricanes Katrina and Maria and the coronavirus disease 2019 (COVID-19) pandemic. U.S. response systems were ill prepared for Hurricane Katrina in 2005; as a result, federal response was stalled, contributing to almost 2,000 fatalities.[18] Although reforms were made to improve response on the basis of lessons learned from the hurricane, over a decade later a similar problem of challenging response unfolded when Hurricane Maria struck the U.S. territory of Puerto Rico, contributing to nearly 3,000 deaths.[19] And a haphazard and disjointed response to the COVID-19 pandemic appears to have contributed to morbidity, mortality, job loss, and other significant damages to households and families.[20] A significant cyber incident will be a novel event. Therefore, we should not necessarily expect that existing incident response processes are

---

[17] Michael K. Lindell, "Disaster Studies," *Current Sociology*, Vol. 61, No. 5–6, 2013.

[18] U.S. House of Representatives, Select Bipartisan Committee to Investigate the Preparation for and Response to Hurricane Katrina, *A Failure of Initiative: Final Report of the Select Bipartisan Committee to Investigate the Preparation for and Response to Hurricane Katrina*, Report 109-377, Washington, D.C.: U.S. Government Printing Office, February 15, 2006.

[19] Nishant Kishore, Domingo Marqués, Ayesha Mahmud, Mathew V. Kiang, Irmary Rodriguez, Arlan Fuller, Peggy Ebner, Cecilia Sorensen, Fabio Racy, Jay Lemery, Leslie Maas, Jennifer Leaning, Rafael A. Irizarry, Satchit Balsari, and Caroline O. Buckee, "Mortality in Puerto Rico after Hurricane Maria," *New England Journal of Medicine*, Vol. 379, No. 2, 2018.

[20] Drew Altman, "Understanding the U.S. Failure on Coronavirus—An Essay by Drew Altman," *BMJ*, Vol. 370, No. 3417, September 2020; Ellen Johnson Sirleaf and Helen Clark, "Report of the Independent Panel for Pandemic Preparedness and Response: Making COVID-19 the Last Pandemic," *The Lancet*, Vol. 398, No. 10295, July 10, 2021; Lucy Wang Halpern, "The Politicization of COVID-19," *American Journal of Nursing*, Vol. 120, No. 11, November 2020.

well suited to ensure a well-coordinated, successful response to a novel event like a significant cyber incident.

Purpose of This Report

The purpose of this report is to support public and private sector stakeholders working to improve response to a significant cyber incident by exploring where incident response plans for non-cyber events can inform preparation for cyber incident response—and where using non-cyber incident response as a template may be counterproductive or lead to ineffective cyber incident response. This exploratory analysis provides preliminary insights to address these considerations and points to areas in need of further research and analysis.

It is particularly timely to address this issue as the Department of Homeland Security's CISA begins work to coordinate more expansive joint planning with other federal agencies, state, local, territorial, and tribal governments, and the private sector.[21] To aid this evolution in planning, this report considers examples of both human-caused and naturally occurring significant incidents that could affect public health and safety, the economy, and national and homeland security. We aim to understand how large-scale, non-cyber incidents, including natural hazards and terrorist attacks, occur; what decisions, capabilities, and mechanisms are required for effective response; and how the differences between these event types can affect these decisions. Our comparison comes from a recognition that responses to significant cyber incidents are comparatively nascent to responses to other hazards, and that there may be processes or procedures and lessons that can be learned from responses to other hazards in other sectors.

The key issues we examine is whether there are distinctions between cyber incidents and other types of emergencies that necessitate a different approach to planning for and conducting response to those incidents. Our purpose is to take a step back to examine this issue and ask:

[21] CISA, 2021.

- What are the similarities and differences between cyber incidents and other incidents in terms of how they occur?
- Given these similarities and differences, how might they affect the types of decisions incident responders have to make, activities that responders need to undertake, and information available to them to inform those decisions and activities?
- Do these distinctions in turn call for a different approach to cyber incident response, or are the current structures, mechanisms, and approaches sufficiently adaptable to account for the distinctions?

In exploring these questions, we seek to provide initial insights and inform discussions among the stakeholders who are responsible in preparing for and responding to cyber incidents in coordination with other stakeholders. These stakeholders include policymakers and incident response planners in federal, state, local, tribal, and territorial governments and private sector representatives. Planners across critical infrastructure sectors, NCFs, and emergency management will also benefit as they examine how to integrate cyber contingency planning into all-hazards plans.

Approach

Our approach is as follows. We first define emergency management and incident response and then highlight key features of non-cyber incidents, focusing in particular on the relationship between the type of incident and the subsequent response and decisionmaking processes. These discussions were developed based on an examination of literature in the fields of terrorism response, emergency management (for natural hazards), public health emergency response, and cybersecurity. Literature was identified through publication databases (e.g., JSTOR, Lexis Uni) using such search terms as "incident response," "response," and "emergency management," in combination with the relevant incident type (e.g., "terrorism"). We reviewed the results of the searches for relevance based on synopses or introductory explanations of the article or book's research objectives. We also supplemented our work with public reporting on incidents and incident timelines, and U.S. government policy and doctrine.

We provide an abstracted view of each incident type to facilitate comparison of different event types, providing two views of each: one focusing on the perspective of the perpetrator (if human-caused) or the incident itself (if naturally occurring), and a second focusing on the perspective of the incident responders. For each incident type, we are specifically interested in examining *significant* incidents, by which we mean those that have the potential to affect national and homeland security, economic security, public health and safety, and that occur at a scale in which the response requires activating elevated forms of coordinated response on the part of government and, where applicable, the private sector, non-governmental organizations (NGOs), and other stakeholders.[22] We explore each of the incident types with real-world examples.

Because the aim of this report is to help inform the response to significant cyber events, we provide a much more detailed picture of the cyber incident life cycle than we do of the other incident types.

We then conduct a cross-incident analysis to identify similarities and differences between the incident types, with particular attention to how each incident type affects incident response and decisionmaking. We compare the incident types in terms of (1) incident origins, identification, and attribution, including the degree of uncertainty surrounding the incident and the availability of advance warning; (2) responder experience and diversity; and (3) decisions required to respond to the incident, such as incident detection, rating severity, mobilizing resources, implementing response plans, and undertaking response activities. We then provide a summary table comparing the incident types across these key variables.

Our focus is on the time period of an emerging incident, initial response, and transition to recovery. We focus particularly on the early phases of the incidents as they are typically the most intensive phases of decisionmaking, when the scope is greatest for mismanagement or error leading to suboptimal outcomes. This is especially important for a cyber incident where the scope of an incident may not be readily apparent.

---

[22] Adapted from the definition and principles for a *significant cyber incident* as presented in White House, Office of the Press Secretary, 2016.

Limitations

We note some important limitations of this report. This analysis builds on expertise and research across the various forms of incidents, but we necessarily had to develop some abstractions from the myriad ways that each type of incident could occur.

Additionally, given the paucity of significant cyber incidents that have warranted large-scale, coordinated U.S. government responses, research and analysis on a real-world response to significant cyber incidents is limited. Our preliminary findings are based on analysis and extrapolation from other past cyber response efforts and response to other types of incidents. The analysis is based on a limited set of incidents and not a comprehensive review of all such incidents of each type.

Although important lessons can be learned from examination of response to past events, and analysis can help us understand how response to unforeseen or novel events can be instructive, this analysis is not a perfect indicator of events or response contingencies that may be experienced in the future.[23] Significant cyber incidents could evolve in highly unpredictable ways, which means that examining the few prior cyber incidents that had serious consequences (though not rising to the level of a "significant cyber incident" as defined in policy) may not fully expose the factors that planners need to account for.

What Is Emergency Management and Incident Response?

Response to a significant cyber incident can be described using terms from emergency management, incident management, and hazard response playbooks and guidance. All of these in some way refer to different ways of dealing with *disaster* or *potential disaster*, which can be understood as a serious

[23] We note that critical work examining other types of hazards and their implications for cyber incidents precedes us—particularly, Paul N. Stockton, *Superstorm Sandy: Implications for Designing a Post–Cyber Attack Power Restoration System*, Laurel, Md.: Johns Hopkins University Applied Physics Laboratory, March 31, 2016.

disruption to communities or normal processes. There are no hard-and-fast rules for identifying a disaster: Some definitions are based on quantified losses to life and property in a limited geographic area, while others take a broader approach, focusing on breakdowns in systems and processes. Likewise, some stakeholders use the terms *emergency*, *incident*, and *catastrophe* interchangeably with a disaster, while others distinguish between these terms. Thus, definitions of such terms as *disaster*, *incident*, and *emergency* frequently vary across different communities in doctrine and in common usage.

These disasters can be dealt with in a variety of ways, typically grouped in phases,[24] including mitigation,[25] such as activities to prevent a disaster from occurring by reducing the severity or frequency of a hazard or by reducing vulnerability; preparation for a hazard, such as developing plans and procedures ahead of a disaster to improve response; response activities undertaken to save lives and prevent damages during an emergency; and recovery activities that seek to restore or improve the systems or activities of a disaster-affected community. They can further be divided into *response*—the act of intervening to prepare, mitigate, respond, and recover, performed by first responders and others—and management, organizing and coordinating the resources of different stakeholders to respond effectively.

Although these phases are widely used across different emergency management communities, the way they are operationalized differs. For instance, some researchers and policymakers frame these phases as part of a disaster management cycle, starting with pre-disaster mitigation before moving to preparedness, response, and recovery, and back to mitigation.[26]

---

24 Different stakeholders may have slightly different versions of these phases. For instance, although the four-phased grouping of mitigation, preparedness, response, and recovery is widely used, FEMA outlines five mission areas consisting of prevention, protection, mitigation, response, and recovery—and, notably, *prevention* specifically refers to terrorist incidents (see FEMA, *National Preparedness Goal*, Washington, D.C., September 2015).

25 Note that *mitigation* is used differently in cybersecurity, which we define as "to make less severe or painful or to cause to become less harsh or hostile" (see Computer Security Resource Center, "Mitigate," webpage, undated).

26 National Academies of Sciences, Engineering and Medicine, *Strengthening the Disaster Resilience of the Academic Biomedical Research Community: Protecting the Nation's*

However, others challenge this cycle, pointing out that phases in the cycle frequently occur concurrently. For instance, mitigation activities can occur during a so-called response phase, and response and recovery often overlap.[27] Others dispute the cyclical dimensions of the emergency management cycle. They argue that disasters change the systems they affect, meaning that recovery is never a return to pre-disaster conditions but rather a move to something new, and that efforts should be made in recovery to "build back better" and prevent re-creating the conditions that led to the disaster in the first place.[28]

These different conceptualizations have implications for how disaster risk is managed. For instance, a nonphased orientation points to the need to develop incident management processes in ways that are cognizant of the multitude of activities beyond emergency response that might occur during a disaster, while an approach that rejects the cyclical nature of the hazard cycle should allow for investments that promote transformation, not just recovery of pre-disaster conditions.[29]

Understanding the broad history of federal emergency management in the United States can help elucidate the differences in how various hazards might be managed by a variety stakeholder groups. The global history of formal response to an emergency is arguably as long as the history of the state—early Greek and Roman response to famine is well documented—and can be seen throughout the history of the United States.[30] Key federal

---

Investment, Washington, D.C.: National Academies Press, 2017.

[27] National Academies of Sciences, Engineering and Medicine, 2017. See also FEMA's capstone doctrine, which states, "Emergency management is collaborative and tiered. It is a system reflective of a continuous cycle, with no definitive beginning or end. Our efforts often overlap and carry over from one phase to the next" (see FEMA, "Pub 1 and Core Values," webpage, undated-b).

[28] Lee Bosher, Ksenia Chmutina, and Dewald van Niekerk, "Stop Going Around in Circles: Towards a Reconceptualisation of Disaster Risk Management Phases," *Disaster Prevention and Management: An International Journal*, Vol. 30, No. 4/5, April 2021.

[29] Bosher, Chmutina, and van Niekerk, 2021.

[30] For a global history of disaster response see Daniel G. Maxwell, and Peter Walker, *Shaping the Humanitarian World*, London: Routledge, 2014. For a history of U.S. disaster response see Patrick S. Roberts, *Disasters and the American State: How Politicians, Bureaucrats, and the Public Prepare for the Unexpected*, Cambridge, United Kingdom:

structures relevant to current U.S. disaster response includes FEMA, established in 1978, and the Incident Command System and National Incident Management System (ICS NIMS), which emerged to address challenges in cross-jurisdictional response to wildfires in California in the 1970s.[31] Disaster management also has a vast network of increasingly professionalized emergency responders. Emergency responders began establishing themselves as a professional response force in the late 19th and early 20th centuries, while emergency managers began professionalizing in the mid-20th century, with, for example, the development of certification bodies, such as the International Association of Emergency Managers, founded in 1952.[32] Paralleling such professionalization is the growth of research and theory of disaster. Research began in the Cold War and is increasingly consolidating as *disaster studies*.[33]

Collectively, these processes play a significant role in U.S. federal incident response. Research, often conducted in collaboration with practitioners, shapes understanding of how to characterize and respond to threats. Research has shown, for example, that impacts can be multidimensional and far-reaching, such as economic, social, and environmental impacts, and are determined by factors related to the *social production of risk*, or social processes that place people and institutions in positions of danger and leave them exposed and vulnerable to hazard.[34] Drawing on this work, researchers

---

Cambridge University Press, 2013; Scott Gabriel Knowles, *The Disaster Experts: Mastering Risk in Modern America*, Philadelphia: University of Pennsylvania Press, 2012; and Stephen Collier and Andrew Lakoff, "The Vulnerability of Vital Systems: How 'Critical Infrastructure' Became a Security Problem," in Myriam Dunn and Kristian S. Kristensen, eds., *The Politics of Securing the Homeland: Critical Infrastructure, Risk and Securitisation*, London: Routledge, 2008, pp. 40–62.

[31] Kimberly S. Stambler and Joseph A. Barbera, "The Evolution of Shortcomings in Incident Command System: Revisions Have Allowed Critical Management Functions to Atrophy," *Journal of Emergency Management*, Weston, Mass., Vol. 13, No. 6, 2015.

[32] International Association of Emergency Managers, "History of IAEM," webpage, undated.

[33] E. L. Quarantelli, "The Early History of the Disaster Research Center," white paper, University of Delaware, undated.

[34] Ben Wisner, Piers Blaikie, Terry Cannon, and Ian Davis, *At Risk: Natural Hazards, People's Vulnerability and Disasters*, London: Routledge, 2004; Ilan Kelman, *Disaster*

and practitioners have focused on mitigation through vulnerability reduction, and they identified a need to reform and improve a wide array of processes, from education and livelihoods to the built environment. Given the far-reaching and social nature of hazard and vulnerability creation, disaster management becomes "everyone's responsibility"—a dispersed product of a multitude of institutional structures. FEMA's whole community approach,[35] ICS NIMS, and the public-private partnerships for critical infrastructure protection are all examples of this approach. The multisectoral and multi-stakeholder nature of incident management can also be seen in the 15 Emergency Support Functions (ESFs) of FEMA's National Response Framework, designed to coordinate federal incident response along different functional areas, which range from transportation (ESF 1) to energy (ESF 12).[36]

A well-managed response to a disaster or incident is one that is efficiently remediated and results in a post-disaster recovery that improves resiliency and avoids re-creating the conditions that generated the disaster in the first place. Crucially, the response must also be equitable in process and outcome and ensure that different people's needs are accounted for in the response and no one is left behind in the recovery process. Effective management requires situational awareness and information-sharing to make sense of the incident and how it can be managed, robust planning, the ability to mobilize resources, coordination between stakeholders involved in the response, and feedback and continual quality improvement. This requires appropriate financial and human resources in the form of plans, people, and money. Although some of these resources can be accessed during a disaster, many need to be established ahead of time as part of preparedness efforts.

These general principles are present across a multitude of incident management processes for different hazardous events, but as we describe in the next sections, they are not necessarily implemented uniformly. This is in part because different hazards have different origins and varying impacts, and stakeholders may be more concerned with certain impacts than others.

by Choice: How Our Actions Turn Natural Hazards into Catastrophes, Oxford, United Kingdom: Oxford University Press, 2020.

35 FEMA, "Whole Community," webpage, last updated October 6, 2020d.

36 FEMA, "National Response Framework," webpage, last updated October 15, 2021.

Some stakeholders are most concerned with loss of life and large-scale property damage, others may be principally concerned with financial damage and reputational risk. Planners and responders may characterize hazards, determine interventions, and assign responsibility differently. As a result, institutional systems to manage risk and respond to these significant incidents may also vary.

Organization of This Report

The remainder of this report consists of four chapters. In Chapter Two, we provide an overview of key features of non-cyber incidents. In Chapter Three, we delve into the life cycle of significant cyber incidents. In Chapter Four, we present our cross-incident analysis. In Chapter Five, we provide our recommendations and identify areas for future research.

CHAPTER TWO

Key Features of Non-Cyber Incidents

In this chapter, we explore key features of various incident types to understand how these incidents emerge, what the response looks like, and what decisions are required to support the response, particularly in the early stages of incident response.

We examine large-scale terrorist attacks, natural hazards (e.g., hurricanes, earthquakes, and wildfires), and public health emergencies. We chose these incident types because they each represent large-scale incidents that would involve multiple government agencies and other stakeholders in their individual response; can affect homeland or national security, the economy, or public health and safety in significant ways (measured in terms of loss of life or economic impact); and, therefore, have the potential to illustrate ways to consider preparing for cyber incident response in useful ways. For each incident type, we discuss a variety of incidents and the impacts that could result; major elements of the response, including challenges; and the kinds of decisions that typically arise during the incident, such as assessing severity and when to mobilize resources in response.

Terrorist Incidents

Terrorism is defined by the Department of Homeland Security as

> any activity involving a criminally unlawful act that is dangerous to human life or potentially destructive of critical infrastructure or key resources, and that appears intended to intimidate or coerce a civilian population, to influence government policy by intimidation or coer-

> cion, or to affect the conduct of a government by mass destruction, assassination, or kidnapping.[1]

Terrorist incidents vary in terms of their perpetrators, methods, targets, and intended and actual impacts.

For purposes of comparing the response to terrorist incidents with other types of significant incidents, such as natural hazards and significant cyber incidents, we will focus principally on terrorist incidents in which the intended or actual impact is *significant* (measured in terms of casualties and damage to property) and the attack is *complex*.[2] Although these types of terrorist incidents—which require a national-level response—are rare in the United States, an evaluation of some of these events (e.g., the terrorist attacks on September 11, 2001 [9/11] and the 2001 anthrax attacks) high-

---

1 Department of Homeland Security, *Strategic Framework for Countering Terrorism and Targeted Violence*, Washington, D.C., September 2019, p. 4. *Terrorism* is separately defined in the Code of Federal Regulations as "the unlawful use of force and violence against persons or property to intimidate or coerce a government, the civilian population, or any segment thereof, in furtherance of political or social objectives" (28 C.F.R. §0.85). According to the FBI,

> Domestic terrorism is the unlawful use, or threatened use, of force or violence by a group or individual based and operating entirely within the United States or Puerto Rico without foreign direction committed against persons or property to intimidate or coerce a government, the civilian population, or any segment thereof in furtherance of political or social objectives. . . . International terrorism involves violent acts or acts dangerous to human life that are a violation of the criminal laws of the United States or any state, or that would be a criminal violation if committed within the jurisdiction of the United States or any state. These acts appear to be intended to intimidate or coerce a civilian population, influence the policy of a government by intimidation or coercion, or affect the conduct of a government by assassination or kidnapping. International terrorist acts occur outside the United States or transcend national boundaries in terms of the means by which they are accomplished, the persons they appear intended to coerce or intimidate, or the locale in which their perpetrators operate or seek asylum (see FBI, "Terrorism 2002–2005," webpage, undated-b).

All these definitions also draw from U.S. Code Title 18, Section 2331, Definitions, amended as of October 3, 2018.

2 Although there is not a clear delineation for a large-scale terror attack, there are attributes of so-called complex coordinated terrorist attacks. Department of Homeland Security, *Planning Considerations: Complex Coordinated Terrorist Attacks*, Washington, D.C., July 2018.

lights how the different characteristics of the incidents, including variations in attack mode, duration, and types of hazards, can present key challenges for decisionmaking at each stage of the response.

Complex Terrorist Incidents Typically Involve a High Degree of Uncertainty, Although Warning Sometimes Occurs

Terrorism is often used to use raise attention for a particular cause or can have a more apocalyptic aim. Knowledge of a terrorist incident emerges either when authorities acquire information warning of an imminent attack or after the perpetrators successfully conduct an attack.

Terrorists can seek to achieve a variety of different outcomes with their attacks—some want to maximize fatalities, others merely want to trigger a significant response to attract attention to their cause.[3] Because terrorists can have different preferences on the type of violence that best achieves their objectives, the nature of the impacts can also vary widely, to include physical destruction, disruption to critical services, economic harms, and loss of life. In addition, attackers sometimes adjust their plans before and even during an incident, or they intentionally select targets and attack modes for which responders are less well prepared. The reciprocal feedback aspects of terrorism incidents, in which the attackers learn and adapt to the defenses and vice versa, present a continuous challenge for prevention and preparedness activities, such as planning, training, and exercises.

Terrorist incidents vary in terms of scale and impact. For example, the 9/11 attacks were notable for their large scale, in terms of the number of fatalities and level of damage incurred and the human and material resources needed to respond. However, other terrorist incidents that required a substantial response have resulted in comparatively few fatalities. The 2001 anthrax attacks—which killed five individuals—involved the contamination of several mail sorting facilities, news agencies, and congressional offices that

[3] For a broader discussion of how terrorists' preferences on the levels of violence sought in attacks vary and have changed over the last several decades, see Brian Michael Jenkins, "New Age of Terrorism," in David Kamien, ed., *McGraw-Hill Homeland Security Handbook*, New York: McGraw Hill, 2006, pp. 117–130.

received anthrax-laced letters and a wide-ranging law enforcement investigation conducted over several years that resulted in thousands of witness interviews and pieces of evidence collected.[4] The impacts of terrorism can also extend beyond the physical damage and lives lost during the incident, particularly because perpetrators seek out attack methods that amplify the effects of the attack, such as by targeting widely used transportation modes.

Terrorist attacks can affect a single location or multiple locations simultaneously, and, in some cases, incident sites can change unexpectedly as attackers alter their location or as the effects of the incident spread. For example, the 9/11 hijackers targeted sites in Washington, D.C., and New York City within an hour of each other. The terrorist attacks in London on July 7, 2005, involved the nearly simultaneous detonation of explosive devices at three locations on the London Underground, followed an hour later by a detonation on a bus in Tavistock Square. Initial reports of the disruptions on the Underground led some to believe that a power surge was to blame. Later reporting indicated that as many as six explosive devices were suspected on the Underground instead of three.[5] In the case of biological attacks, contagious agents can spread as infected victims travel, resulting in no determined or defined incident site.

The Many Uncertainties Surrounding Terrorist Incidents Pose Challenges for Responders

The many uncertainties surrounding terrorist incidents mean that preparedness for response may not be adequate, even for localities that have prior experience with them. In the period *before* a terrorist incident occurs, federal and SLTT authorities and private companies that may be the target of an attack take measures to prevent and prepare for such events. Preven-

4 The FBI describes the 2001 anthrax investigation, code-named Amerithrax, as "one of the largest and most complex in the history of law enforcement." It reportedly involved 10,000 witness interviews on six different continents, the execution of 80 searches, the recovery of more than 6,000 items, issuance of more than 5,750 grand jury subpoenas, and the collection of 5,730 environmental samples from 60 site locations (see FBI, "Famous Cases and Criminals: Amerithrax or Anthrax Investigation," webpage, undated-a).

5 "Tube Log Shows Initial Confusion," *BBC News*, July 12, 2005.

tion activities and physical security are primarily aimed at disrupting plots before they materialize through law enforcement and intelligence activities that seek to identify the perpetrators and precursor activities common to terrorist attack planning. Such activities can provide advance warning of terrorists' plans and capabilities and help responders prioritize threat scenarios that present the greatest risk. Preparedness activities, in contrast, seek to develop capabilities to respond to terrorism incidents and mitigate their consequence, should they occur.

However, because large-scale terrorist attacks occur infrequently, the scale of such events—when they do occur—can present significant challenges for responders. Responders must be prepared for a wide variety of potential impacts and hazards and can often be thrust into roles for which they may not have been properly prepared or equipped.

For example, responders who participated in rescue operations at the 9/11 attack sites indicated that available personal protective equipment and training practices were not designed to protect from the variety of hazards they encountered, including "burning fuel, hazardous materials, structures prone to collapse, heat stress, exhaustion, and respiratory irritants."[6] In addition, emergency response equipment and procedures are generally designed for situations that last for short periods of time, not days and weeks. This meant that during the 9/11 response, protective equipment was not available in sufficient quantities to match the scale of the problem or was ill-suited for the nature of the response.[7]

When attackers target multiple sites simultaneously, response operations might need to be conducted over a multijurisdictional, multistate region. Investigations of terrorism incidents, including efforts to identify and apprehend individuals participating in or supporting the attack, are likely to cross state and international boundaries and require coordination with

---

6 Brian A. Jackson, D. J. Peterson, James T. Bartis, Tom LaTourrette, Irene T. Brahmakulam, Ari Houser, and Jerry M. Sollinger, *Protecting Emergency Responders: Lessons Learned from Terrorist Attacks*, Santa Monica, Calif.: RAND Corporation, CF-176-OSTP, 2002, p. 11.

7 Emergency responders reported that equipment did not provide sufficient protection against the heat of fires at the sites and the demanding physical environment of unstable rubble piles, nor were they light and flexible enough to allow workers to move debris and enter confined spaces (see Jackson et al., 2002, p. xi).

a host of federal, local, and international law enforcement authorities, particularly when attacks are planned by actors outside the United States.

The timing of an incident and the potential for multiple attacks can also pose challenges for responders. Terrorists can choose to attack at a time when response personnel are preoccupied or inadequately prepared to respond. Some attack modes may result in delayed effects, making it more difficult for responders to evaluate the severity of the incident and to appropriately direct response actions. In addition, concerns that the perpetrators may conduct follow-on attacks, including against first responders at the attack site, may cause delays in the response until the incident site is sufficiently protected against such attacks. In some situations, the cascading impacts of an attack can disrupt critical services beyond the attack site, which can indirectly undermine the response. For example, the grounding of commercial air transport following the 9/11 attacks reportedly slowed the implementation of command and logistical support infrastructures assisting that response.[8]

The duration of terrorist incidents can also vary depending on the mode of the attack and the effectiveness of the response—particularly if the perpetrators remain at large. Incidents resulting in contaminated sites are likely to prolong a response, particularly if appropriate personal protective equipment and capabilities to deal with hazardous materials are not available in the jurisdiction. For example, the 2001 anthrax attacks consisted of a series of biohazard incidents involving cases of real contamination, false alarms, and hoaxes over the course of several months.[9] Another factor that could prolong a response is that the incident site is also a crime scene and investigators are likely to carefully collect evidence only after they can safely access the site. The responses to the 9/11 attacks involved years of constant work, including an initial urgent phase at the attack sites focused on search and rescue and collection of evidence for investigation and prosecution that persisted for several days and then gradually transitioned into a sustained

[8] Jackson et. al., 2002, p. x.

[9] FBI, undated; "Timeline: How the Anthrax Terror Unfolded," National Public Radio, February 15, 2011.

campaign to clean up the sites and conduct a criminal investigation of the perpetrators that lasted long after the attacks.[10]

Responders Must Often Make Decisions Based on Incomplete Information

The challenges we have just described, including high degree of uncertainty surrounding terrorist incidents, mean that responders must often make decisions and act rapidly, and often based on an imperfect understanding of the nature and severity of the event. Responders can come from the local, state, and federal levels, and the nature of the decisionmaking process and the key players in the response will vary depending on the type of incident and whether it begins with a warning or a direct attack.

If a terrorist incident begins with receipt of threat information warning of an impending attack, federal agencies will evaluate the credibility and severity of the threat and tailor the response accordingly.[11] Such analysis will most immediately inform law enforcement actions, led by the FBI, that are aimed at preventing and resolving the threat, particularly by identifying, locating, and arresting the perpetrators.[12] The level of concern increases significantly if the attack method can result in significant consequences, particularly if there is potential for the use of chemical, biological, radiological, or nuclear (CBRN) weapons. In such cases, response actors may initiate plans to mitigate the consequence of such incidents should they occur, including the use of federal resources to augment state and local capabilities and proposition resources, particularly if the threat information provides details of potential locations and targets for the incident.[13] Additionally,

---

[10] Work to identify victim remains continued for more than a decade after the attacks. Jackson et al., 2022, p. x.; and Melanie Eversley, "12 Years After, WTC Debris Still Sifted for Remains," *USA Today*, April 6, 2013.

[11] For more detail on how federal law enforcement agencies assess the credibility and severity of threat information during an terrorism incident, see Department of Justice and the Federal Bureau of Investigation, *National Response Plan: Terrorism Incident Law Enforcement and Investigation Annex*, Washington, D.C., December 2004.

[12] Department of Justice and the Federal Bureau of Investigation, 2004, pp. TER-11.

[13] Department of Justice and the Federal Bureau of Investigation, 2004, pp. TER-11.

responders have to be postured for additional attacks; they cannot assume that the initial attack is going to be the only incident. Federal and state governments may also release information about the threat to the public to encourage them to share information on suspicious activity and take preparatory actions to mitigate the consequence of the incident.[14]

Such periods of pre-incident response activities are often characterized by rapid and wide-ranging investigative actions on the basis of limited and fragmentary information aimed at unraveling the plot. For example, the FBI launched a sweeping investigation following the arrest of Ahmed Ressam (the so-called Millennium Bomber) in 1999—who was detained while attempting to enter the United States from Canada with an explosive device—based on intelligence warning of additional plots in the United States and abroad.[15] In a matter of days, the FBI reportedly placed hundreds of suspects under surveillance across the country and subsequently arrested a suspect who authorities were concerned was planning to target a New Year's Eve celebration in Seattle.[16]

If a terrorist attack occurs without warning, local first responders are often the first to arrive at the attack site and must evaluate the severity of the incident and determine how to proceed. The initial response will seek to preserve life, minimize further risks to health, and prevent the threatening act from causing additional harms. Local first responders must quickly evaluate whether they—based on their initial assessment of the nature of the event—possess sufficient resources to manage the response or if they should initiate emergency response procedures to request additional resource from state and federal agencies. It can be difficult to fully appreciate the severity of the incident during this initial response period.

---

14 The Department of Homeland Security administers a formal process to release threat information to the public (see Department of Homeland Security, National Terrorism Advisory System," webpage, undated-a).

15 Josh Meyer, "Border Arrest Stirs Fear of Terrorist Cells in U.S.," *Los Angeles Times*, March 11, 2001.

16 Frontline, "Other Millennium Attacks," webpage, undated; and Hal Bernton, Mike Carter, David Heath, and James Neff, "The Terrorist Within: The Story Behind One Man's Holy War Against America," *Seattle Times*, June 23–July 7, 2002.

For conventional attack methods, such as bombings, the impacts are immediate, but the motivation for the incident may be unclear. For example, it can be difficult to initially know whether an explosion was caused by an accident, criminals, or terrorists. For unconventional attack methods, such as biological attacks, the impacts may not be recognized until days later, particularly for agents with long incubation periods. Following the 2001 anthrax attacks, first responders later described their difficulties in assessing the significance of the incident because they initially did not know what the "invisible hazards" were or where they were located.[17] After this attack, identifying such attacks actually became more difficult rather than less difficult, as so-called *white powder incidents* involving the mailing of benign substances that look like anthrax powder became exceedingly common, and more than 50,000 such incidents were reported within a year of the attacks.[18] Such "faux terrorism" incidents often require similar responses as actual threats until the substances can be tested. The frequency of such incidents may encourage first responders to lower their guard, affecting their decisionmaking during an actual threat.

The Response to a Terrorist Attack Requires Close Coordination Among Multiple Functions and Levels of Government

When a terrorist attack occurs, coordination among law enforcement, criminal investigators, protective activities, and emergency management functions across all levels of government needs to occur rapidly to keep pace with a quickly unfolding situation.

If an incident is believed to be an act of terrorism or if the resources required to manage the event outstrip local capabilities, local authorities can notify state and federal agencies to request assistance. A decision of whether to expand the response depends in large part on a judgment (coor-

---

[17] Jackson et al., 2002, p. 16.

[18] As of 2012, there are more than 800 white powder incidents reported across the country every year, often involving baking soda, sugar, ground-up antacids, corn starch, baby powder, or dried toothpaste. Yudhijit Bhattacharjees, "The Curse of the White Powder," *Slate*, January 30, 2012

dinated between federal and local responders) of whether terrorism is the cause of the incident and whether the potential harms are significant (e.g., involving CBRN materials).[19] In such cases, the FBI, in coordination with local authorities, would oversee the law enforcement response, including working to identify and apprehend the perpetrators and gathering evidence to support prosecution.[20] FEMA, along with state and local consequence management agencies, would focus on alleviating the damage, protecting public health, and restoring essential services.

Summary

- Terrorist incidents emerge either when authorities acquire information warning of an imminent attack or after the perpetrators successfully conduct an attack. Strategic and tactical warning is critical to disruption, mitigation, and response to terrorist plots.
- Large-scale terrorist incidents typically involve a high degree of uncertainty in terms of physical destruction, disruption to critical services, economic harms, and loss of life. Incidents can vary in terms of scale and impact, and can sometimes involve multiple locations or cascading effects.
- A terrorist is a thinking adversary and disruption may, in some cases, only delay, mitigate, or cause the targets to shift.
- The many uncertainties surrounding terrorist incidents mean that preparedness for response may not be adequate, even for localities that have prior experience with them. The timing of an incident and the potential for multiple attacks can also pose challenges.
- Responders to terrorist incidents must act rapidly, and therefore often need to make decisions based on incomplete information. The early moments after a terrorist incident can be confusing because authori-

19 For more information detailing FEMA's guidance to state and local authorities related to developing emergency operational procedures in response to terrorism incidents, including weapons of mass destruction events, see FEMA, *Managing the Emergency Consequences of Terrorist Incidents: Interim Planning Guide for State and Local Governments*, Washington, D.C., July 2002.

20 FEMA, 2002.

ties not only have to assess the impact of the event but also must be postured to respond to additional attacks.

- Responders can come from the local, state, and federal levels, and the nature of the decisionmaking process and the key players in the response will vary depending on whether an incident begins with a warning or a direct attack. The response to an attack requires close coordination among multiple functions and levels of government.

Natural Hazards

The United States is subject to a variety of natural hazards that are capable of producing large-scale emergencies and disasters. Although some natural hazards, such as flooding,[21] impact virtually every part of the country, many natural hazards capable of producing extreme impacts vary based on the region of the country and its underlying geography.[22] Some regions are subject to multiple natural threats and hazards, putting these areas at greater risk and creating greater burdens on emergency management.[23]

Climate change is increasing the frequency and intensity of many natural hazards.[24] Although the largest, most-damaging, and most-difficult-to-manage natural hazards, such as major hurricanes and large earthquakes, occur with less frequency, even smaller versions of these events can produce severe local impacts. In addition, as demonstrated by the COVID-19 pandemic, even low-probability or infrequent events can be expected at some point in time. Accordingly, it is only a matter of time until a large rare event, such as a major earthquake, will affect the United States.

---

[21] National Severe Storms Laboratory, "Severe Weather 101—Floods," webpage, undated.

[22] Red Cross, "Common Disasters Across the U.S.," webpage, undated.

[23] FEMA's national risk index shows vulnerability to natural hazards at the county level across the continental United States (see FEMA, "National Risk Index," webpage, undated-a).

[24] U.S. Geological Survey, "Frequently Asked Questions: How Can Climate Change Affect Natural Disasters?" webpage, undated-b.

The impact of natural hazards can be tremendous. In 2020 alone, the United States experienced 22 weather- and climate-related disasters that each generated costs exceeding $1 billion.[25] These events included a variety of natural hazard types, such as hurricanes, wildfires, derecho events, and severe weather and flooding. Although 2020 did not see a billion-dollar-damage event from an earthquake or tsunami, these natural hazards are equally capable of producing damages of this magnitude.

Natural Hazards Vary in Scope and Impact Though Some Types of Hazards Occur with Regularity

The duration of the disaster event itself may be limited to minutes, such as when a major earthquake strikes, or may unfold over hours, days, or weeks, as in the case of hurricanes, flooding, and wildfires. Although the intensity and frequency of natural hazards experienced in a region varies in any given year, regions are generally subject to the same natural hazards year to year. Natural hazards typically affect areas based on underlying geographic characteristics, such as elevation or proximity to a fault line or coastal area, making it possible to identify natural hazard exposure with a relatively high degree of fidelity.[26]

Natural hazards can have a variety of impacts on people, critical infrastructure, property, and the natural environment. Common life safety concerns in the immediate aftermath of a natural hazard include drowning and injuries and death caused by collapsed infrastructure.

Damages typically diminish with distance from the origin point of the incident, but are also related to the underlying geography of an area and factors in the built environment, including the quality of building construction, the adequacy of drainage, and the availability of protective measures and mitigation, such as levees. Other factors, such as shifting winds, may similarly influence how natural hazards affect areas. As a result, it is not uncommon that damage may vary greatly even within the same neighborhood. Similarly, the timing of a natural hazard can be a significant factor in

25 National Oceanic and Atmospheric Administration, "Billion-Dollar Weather and Climate Disasters: Overview," webpage, undated.

26 California Office of Emergency Services, "My Hazards," webpage, undated.

its impacts, particularly for such no-notice events as earthquakes. Natural hazards that occur overnight are likely to occur while more individuals are home and may be asleep, as opposed to being in a densely populated city center or using mass transit. This can either exacerbate or reduce injuries and deaths. Flooding and high water are more difficult to assess at night and may create additional hazards for motorists and responders.

Some disasters may threaten life safety for weeks after their immediate impact by spreading illness and disease through contaminated flood waters. Medically fragile individuals may be at risk for significant periods following these disasters if medical facilities are damaged, inaccessible, or overwhelmed or if power is not available for in-home medical devices, heating, or cooling systems. Exposure can also result in mental trauma, particularly if appropriate health services or resources are unavailable.

The largest types of natural disasters, such as major hurricanes, earthquakes, and tsunamis, can affect multistate regions.[27] Because these disasters can affect such critical infrastructure as roads, bridges, and power generation and distribution equipment, these events can affect areas far from the primary impact site, creating cascading economic, transportation, and other effects. They can also lead to the release of hazardous materials or ruptured gas lines, which can create dangerous fires. They can harm the natural environment directly by eroding coast lines, destroying natural habits for wildlife, and releasing contaminants, and indirectly by creating massive amounts of debris that can only be disposed of in landfills. In addition, the evacuation of large numbers of people and the destruction of facilities, such as hospitals, can create additional strains on areas that were not directly affected by the hazard.

The magnitude of natural hazards, such as earthquakes, hurricanes, and tornadoes, are assessed using widely known severity scales. However, these scales refer to the magnitude of the underlying natural phenomena (e.g., maximum sustained windspeed). As a result, they can provide only a general indication of the potential impact of the natural hazard. Although, in general terms, larger natural hazards are capable of producing greater impacts than smaller ones (for the reasons discussed above), actual impacts

[27] FEMA, "Historic Disasters," webpage, last updated January 4, 2022.

are likely to vary significantly even for events of the same size based on several underlying human and natural factors, only some of which are possible to predict or control.[28]

The Response to Natural Disasters Can Vary Based on the Availability of Advance Warning

Although regions are exposed to a known variety of natural hazards, the amount of advance warning available for an individual acute incident varies by hazard. Some events, such as earthquakes, may occur with essentially no notice, making public warning and advanced preparation for a specific event beyond general planning impossible.[29] The initial response to a no-notice disaster, such as a tornado or earthquake, is likely to be initiated by calls to 911 immediately following the event, and it will primarily be conducted by local resources. Volunteers and bystanders might begin to assist victims to the extent they are capable of doing so. Response will begin in earnest when outdoor conditions are safe enough for response by police, fire, emergency medical services, and more-specialized responders.

A primary challenge for emergency managers in no-notice events is understanding the scope and magnitude of the event and developing and mobilizing an organized response. The initial priority will be given to life safety, followed by a more comprehensive damage assessment effort to identify damage to critical infrastructure and, finally, to private property.

For no-notice events, such as earthquakes, the likely areas in which they would occur mean that local ordinances (e.g., construction codes) and preparedness can focus on shoring up mitigations against those hazards, even when the exact timing, location, and severity of the event cannot be

---

[28] U.S. Geological Survey, "Frequently Asked Questions: Why Do Earthquakes in Other Countries Seem to Cause More Damage and Casualties Than Earthquakes in the U.S.?" webpage, undated-c.

[29] Earthquake early warning is available through the Earthquake Early Warning System and ShakeAlert, which provides warning of an earthquake of several seconds to potentially a few minutes, depending on the distance from the earthquake epicenter. This amount of warning means that any actions are likely to be taken by individuals to seek cover and allow responders to be aware of an impending earthquake (U.S. Geological Survey, "Early Warning," webpage, undated-a).

predicted. Most often, however, prevention or disruption is not a realistic option, which makes preparedness and swift response critical.

Other events, such as major hurricanes, can be forecast several days in advance of landfall, with increasing precision regarding magnitude, timing and likely area affected. Warning of a natural hazard allows for a variety of preparedness and protective activities to occur in advance, including voluntary or mandatory evacuation, prepositioning of resources, activation of emergency plans and emergency operations centers (EOCs), and request for and receipt of mutual aid resources from non-affected jurisdictions, or aid from the federal government.[30]

Preparation for these disasters may include developing detailed hazard-specific emergency plans, establishing evacuation routes, purchasing and prepositioning equipment, and conducting drills and exercises. Individuals and families may be encouraged to develop personal emergency plans and purchase needed supplies and resources to mitigate the potential impacts of these disasters in their area.[31] Response will begin in earnest when conditions outside are safe enough for response by police, fire, emergency medical services, and more-specialized responders.

For either type of incident, even when the span of the actual event may be brief, response activities may occur over days or weeks for large-scale events. For example, response to a major earthquake may require search and rescue activities for days following the actual earthquake, and response to unstable buildings, fires, and hazardous-materials leaks for a week after the event.

Incidents of especially large magnitude create additional burdens on the emergency response system, often requiring out-of-state or out-of-region resources to be drawn in for mutual aid. This can create difficulties for emergency management, including increased arrival time for resources or difficulty integrating resources into EOC systems. FEMA has created several tools to facilitate standardization of response among emergency managers, such as resource typing and the National Incident Management System,

---

[30] National Hurricane Program, "Hurrevac," webpage, undated.

[31] FEMA, *Are You Ready? An In-Depth Guide to Citizen Preparedness*, Washington, D.C., P-2064, September 2020a.

which are expressly designed to facilitate the integration of resources from disparate locations.[32]

Although most natural hazards cannot be prevented, failure to respond adequately, particularly to predictable events or those which occur with warning, can undermine faith in government.

The Availability of Advance Warning Also Influences Decisionmaking

The availability of advance warning also influences the types of decisions to be made during response to a natural disaster. For example, in the case of a hurricane, the advance warning period and the existence of a well-known severity scale enable emergency management officials to plan their response, including requesting and prepositioning resources (e.g., swift water rescue teams) and activating and staffing their EOCs. Advanced warning disasters also allow elected officials to declare a state of emergency prior to the event. Depending on state and local laws, this might activate emergency powers that are not otherwise available; in addition, declaring a state of emergency sends a strong public warning and may be accompanied by specific instructions to the public, including the evacuation of an area that is expected to be heavily affected by the event or an order for residents to shelter in place. For such repetitive hazards as flooding and hurricanes, when conditions are safe enough, authorities may also initiate proactive surveys of areas that are known to be commonly affected, such as flood-prone areas.

In contrast, a primary challenge for emergency managers in no-notice events is developing situational awareness of the scope and magnitude of the event to mobilize an organized response. Emergency managers will perform some of the same actions as in an incident with some advance notice, such as activating the emergency operations, declaring a state of emergency if the event is large enough, requesting and deploying specialized resources, and providing direction to the public. However, any of these actions may be made more difficult as a result of their occurring *after* the primary impact

---

[32] Department of Homeland Security, "Resource Typing Library Tool," online catalogue, version 1.6.11, undated-b; and FEMA, *National Incident Management System, Third Edition*, Washington, D.C., October 2017.

of the event. For example, in the case of a major earthquake, emergency management officials and first responders could themselves be injured by the event and unable to report for duty, such key facilities as EOCs may be damaged or inoperable, and transportation routes may be blocked. No-notice disasters that occur overnight may present particular problems for an emergency response. Among other challenges, officials may have difficulty developing situational awareness of the scope of the event and the scale and nature of its impacts on people, critical infrastructure, and property until conditions allow for visual inspection and search and rescue.

Summary

- Incident response to natural hazards varies depending on the type of hazard, but many natural hazards, although unpredictable in their individual paths, are known hazards, and the response capabilities and capacity required are well documented and tracked.
- Emergency responders include both volunteers and bystanders helping in the immediate wake of a disaster; professional emergency management personnel, including policy, fire, and emergency medical personnel; and more-specialized responders.
- There are commonly accepted means of assessing severity of many natural hazards, which directly informs the forms and scale of response.
- When a natural hazard, such as a hurricane, occurs, there is often sufficient warning to preposition response capabilities, warn the population and initiate evacuations from the areas likely to be affected, and mobilize authorities and resources.
- For no-notice events, such as earthquakes, the likely areas in which they would occur means that local ordinances (e.g., construction codes) and preparedness can focus more on shoring up mitigations against those hazards, even when the exact timing, location, and severity of the event cannot be predicted. Most often, however, prevention or disruption is not a realistic option, which makes preparedness and swift response critical.
- The availability of advance warning also influences decisionmaking. A primary challenge for emergency managers in no-notice events is

developing situational awareness of the scope and magnitude of the event to mobilize an organized response. When advance warning is available, as in the case of a hurricane, emergency management officials can plan their response in advance, including requesting and prepositioning resources and activating and staffing their EOCs.

Public Health Emergencies

Public health emergencies are incidents with the potential to severely compromise the health of a community or a group of people, resulting in morbidity or mortality and lowered well-being.[33] As long as they can potentially compromise health, various incidents can cause and be classified as public health emergencies under this definition, including natural hazards, such as floods and hurricanes; terrorist attacks; technological disasters, such as oil spills; and disease outbreaks. Along with being public health emergencies, many of these incidents can also fall into other categories (e.g., natural hazard, terrorist attack). However, managing the public health effects of these incidents requires unique response capabilities and mechanisms—therefore, we discuss them separately here, covering a breadth of incidents, including disease outbreaks, natural hazards, and technological disasters to illustrate the phases, impacts, and decisionmaking processes contained within public health incident management.

---

[33] An alternative definition focuses on the organizational nature of emergencies, defining *public health emergencies* as when "health consequences have the potential to overwhelm routine community capabilities to address them" (see Christopher Nelson, Nicole Lurie, Jeffrey Wasserman, and Sarah Zakowski, "Conceptualizing and Defining Public Health Emergency Preparedness," *American Journal of Public Health*, Vol. 97, Suppl. 1, 2007). For a discussion on the organizational definition of public health emergency see Andrew Lakoff, *Unprepared: Global Health in a Time of Emergency*, Oakland, Calif.: University of California Press, 2017.

Variation Exists in the Characteristics, Impacts, and Duration of a Public Health Emergency

Tremendous variation exists in the stages that occur prior to a public health emergency, in the spread and impact of the emergency, whether the emergency can be forecast, and in the typical duration of a public health emergency. Triggers for some health emergencies, such as the 2010 Haiti earthquake that led to an estimated 200,000 deaths, occur suddenly or with limited warning. Others, such as the 2011 East Africa drought, the ongoing U.S. opioid crisis, and most hurricanes, can be identified in advance or evolve gradually and slowly into a public health emergency.

Depending on the nature of the emergency and its response, public health disasters can result in secondary cascading disasters, disrupting livelihoods and economic systems, supply chains, and potentially compromising other infrastructure and critical lifelines. Examples of recent public health emergencies within the United States include the ongoing opioid crisis; 2021 winter storms in Texas; 2020 California and Oregon wildfires; and hurricanes in Florida, Georgia, and North Carolina; and, of course, the COVID-19 pandemic, which, as of April 2022, had resulted in 79 million cases and 979,000 deaths in the United States.[34]

Several Features of Public Health Emergencies Make Response Challenging

Although public health emergencies can be caused by a wide variety of incidents, events, and phenomena, as they emerge, these emergencies share some common characteristics that make response challenging.

First, public health emergencies can be characterized by significant uncertainty in terms of their cause, vectors, or impacts. This can make it difficult to identify effective mitigation strategies and countermeasures. For instance, death tolls from Hurricane Maria were initially estimated to be 50, but this figure grew, with estimates ranging between 800 and 8,500 deaths

[34] Department of Health and Human Services, "Public Health Emergency Declarations," webpage, last updated March 14, 2022. COVID-19 data are from the Centers for Disease Control and Prevention, "COVID-19," webpage, undated.

due both to the hurricane and its impact on critical infrastructure.[35] The official death toll was eventually calculated at 3,000.[36] Uncertainty around disease outbreaks can be even higher, because it is often difficult initially to classify new outbreaks and identify the disease, and then understand the spread, scope, morbidity, and mortality; effective medical and nonmedical countermeasures; and public health communication strategies for novel diseases. COVID-19 is a recent example of this. During the pandemic's initial stages, public health officials and medical personnel did not understand many aspects of the disease, such as how it spread and what interventions and treatments would be most effective, resulting in slow responses and an emphasis on initial interventions (such as cleaning surfaces) that later were identified as less effective. HIV and AIDS are other examples. When the virus and the resulting disease were first discovered, there was a high level of uncertainty about its causes, rate of spread, prevention options, and mechanisms for response. Even classifying whether something is a public health emergency can be challenging. For instance, the ongoing opioid crisis has been labeled a health disaster necessitating targeted emergency response,[37] but other health events with large negative impacts (e.g., obesity, smoking) are not classified as public health emergencies.

Second is the large number of often inexperienced stakeholders who respond to public health emergencies. As with natural hazards, public health emergencies often involve spontaneous and emergent forms of response with members of the public, community groups, and individuals and households frequently pitching in to protect themselves and their neighbors.[38] But

---

[35] Kishore et al., 2018.

[36] Central Office for Recovery, Reconstruction and Resiliency, *Transformation and Innovation in the Wake of Devastation: An Economic and Disaster Recovery Plan for Puerto Rico*, August 8, 2018.

[37] President Donald J. Trump declared the opioid crisis a public health emergency on October 26, 2017 (see Centers for Medicare and Medicaid Services, "Ongoing Emergencies & Disasters," webpage, last modified December 1, 2021).

[38] Thomas E. Drabek, and David A. McEntire, "Emergent Phenomena and the Sociology of Disaster: Lessons, Trends and Opportunities from the Research Literature," *Disaster Prevention and Management: An International Journal*, Vol. 12, No. 2, 2003; John Twigg and Irina Mosel, "Emergent Groups and Spontaneous Volunteers in Urban Disaster Response," *Environment and Urbanization*, Vol. 29, No. 2, 2017; Daniela G.

unlike response to natural hazards, where an established cadre of full-time professional emergency managers and responders (e.g., firefighters, incident managers) complements these emergent responders, the class of responders with the professional expertise required for public health disasters are also often inexperienced in disaster response, including public health departments, hospitals, epidemiologists, and other health professionals. Many of these public health responders are dual-hatted—for example, when an emergency strikes, they must rapidly shift from their non-emergency positions to respond to the disaster.[39] As a result, they may have less training, less experience with emergency management policy (such as ICS NIMS), and are less well prepared to shift to an emergency response mentality than full-time emergency managers and responders.[40] This professional culture is at odds with many of the features of public health emergency response, which occurs under conditions of uncertainty, during which responders often lack relevant training, expertise, and strong evidence that can guide decisionmaking.[41]

Investing in public health emergency preparedness (PHEP) is intended to address many of these challenges. *PHEP* is "the capability of the public health and health care systems, communities, and individuals to prevent, protect

---

Domínguez, Dellanira García, David A. Martínez, and Belinda Hernandez-Arriaga, "Leveraging the Power of Mutual Aid, Coalitions, Leadership, and Advocacy During COVID-19," *American Psychologist*, Vol. 75, No. 7, October 2020.

39 D. A. Rose, S. Murthy, J. Brooks, and J. Bryant, "The Evolution of Public Health Emergency Management as a Field of Practice," *American Journal of Public Health*, Vol. 107, No. S2, September 2017; Matthew W. Lewis, Edward W. Chan, Christopher Nelson, Andrew Hackbarth, Christine Anne Vaughan, Alonzo L. Plough, and Brit K. Oiulfstad, "Wearing Many Hats: Lessons About Preparedness and Routine Public Health from the H1n1 Response," in M. Stoto and M Higdon, eds., *The Public Health Response to 2009 H1N1: A Systems Perspective*, Oxford, United Kingdom: Oxford University Press, 2015.

40 Lewis et al., 2015.

41 Bringing together public health officials and emergency managers to prepare for public health emergencies can help address this condition, but still requires a change in perspective for those who are not conditioned to think in terms of emergency response. This change will take time and habitual practice. For one example of a state's approach to this, see Commonwealth of Massachusetts, "Office of Preparedness and Emergency Management," website, undated.

against, quickly respond to, and recover from health emergencies,"[42] and includes such activities as pre-disaster planning and training and broader mitigation targeted at reducing community vulnerability and improving well-being. Maintaining preparedness requires ongoing resources, and, although significant resources were invested in PHEP following 9/11 and the 2001 anthrax attacks and again after the H1N1 swine flu pandemic in 2009,[43] there have also been long periods of underinvestment in PHEP and subsequent reduction in preparedness throughout the United States.[44]

Uncertainty Surrounding the Nature of the Incident Itself Can Complicate Decisionmaking in Response to a Public Health Emergency

Public health emergency response typically requires rapid decisionmaking, which many public health professionals may find unfamiliar, as the field's professional culture emphasizes deliberation, debate, and careful gathering of scientific evidence for analysis.[45] (The response to the COVID-19 pandemic may have changed this dynamic to some extent, but whether this change will endure remains to be seen.) For slowly emerging emergencies, early warning and early action mechanisms can be put in place to identify public health hazards as they emerge and to intervene before they can turn into emergency.[46] These mechanisms are not effective for hazards that immediately result in significant public health impacts, and they require

---

42 Nelson et al., 2007.

43 Nelson et al., 2007; Ryan Ellis, *Letters, Power Lines, and Other Dangerous Things: The Politics of Infrastructure Security*, Cambridge, Mass.: MIT Press, 2020.

44 Nason Maani and Sandro Galea, "COVID-19 and Underinvestment in the Public Health Infrastructure of the United States," *Milbank Quarterly*, Vol. 98, No. 2, June 2020, p. 250; and Trust for America's Health, *The Impact of Chronic Underfunding on America's Public Health System: Trends, Risks, and Recommendations, 2020*, Washington, D.C.: April 2020.

45 Daniel J. Barnett, George S. Everly Jr., Cindy L. Parker, and Jonathan M. Links, "Applying Educational Gaming to Public Health Workforce Emergency Preparedness," *American Journal of Preventive Medicine*, Vol. 28, No. 4, 2005

46 International Federation of Red Cross and Red Crescent Societies, *Early Warning, Early Action: Mechanisms for Rapid Decision-Making*, Geneva, Switzerland, July 2014.

decisionmaking processes that favor interventions to address hazards before they become emergencies.

The first steps in any public health response are to identify the incident, determine whether it is a public health emergency, and decide whether and how to respond. Identification can be challenging, given the uncertainties that surround public health incidents. It can occur through an existing early warning and monitoring system (if the health hazard can be predicted in advance and if a monitoring system in place), or as part of an unfolding identification based on tacit knowledge and professional expertise, a process known as *sensemaking*. In most places, identification of potential threats is a part of routine surveillance and monitoring, most threats identified are minor, and decisions are made to continue normal operations and monitoring. However, occasionally events can signal that a routine one may become overwhelmed. This may lead to a decision to activate a partial or full public health response.

With the initial public health emergency identified, efforts are then put in place to develop appropriate response procedures, which would include collecting data to identify the scope of the problem and determine necessary medical and nonmedical countermeasures. Response organizations—which could include public health departments and/or emergency management agencies—might set up an incident management system to coordinate the response. The incident management team would work with those responding to the emergency (e.g., frontline responders, such as public and private hospitals, and emergency response NGOs), specialized hazard-specific response agencies (e.g., wildland fire departments for wildfires), and broader organizations playing a role in a response (e.g., schools, restaurants, grocery stores, or community-based organizations).

Several federal guiding documents outline what the response should entail, notably FEMA's ESF No. 8 (which focuses on public health and medical services).[47] The ESF outlines key capacities for response—specifically, planning, operational coordination, and public information and warning. It designates the Department of Health and Human Services as the coordinator and lead agency for overseeing these response processes, lists other

[47] FEMA, "Emergency Support Function #8–Public Health and Medical Services Annex," June 2016.

agencies as support (including the Departments of Agriculture, Commerce, Defense, Energy, and Homeland Security), and defines the roles for SLTT governments and other partners. Significantly, it identifies the private sector as critical to response, stating that "[t]he vast majority of public health and medical activities and services are provided by the private health care sector. ESF #8 augments the support provided by the private health care sector."[48] At the local community level, service providers and organizations that facilitate access to essential health services are also crucial, particularly for vulnerable and marginalized populations and for communicating with the public using appropriate communication mechanisms and channels.[49]

As the emergency unfolds, ongoing adjustments are made in response to its evolving impact and the effectiveness of interventions. Impacts are often measured by current and projected morbidity and mortality (receiving less attention but also important are the mental and behavioral health impacts associated with the emergency).[50] And as with other emergencies, impacts differ between population groups, with vulnerable and marginalized populations (populations with preexisting health conditions or challenges in accessing essential health services or communicating with providers) typically being most affected. These differential impacts must be accounted for and incorporated into the response through targeted population-specific interventions that ensure equity in response outcomes.[51] Adjustments are

48 FEMA, 2016.

49 Matthew W. Seeger, Laura E. Pechta, Simani M. Price, Keri M. Lubell, Dale A. Rose, Saloni Sapru, Melanie C. Chansky, and Belinda J. Smith, "A Conceptual Model for Evaluating Emergency Risk Communication in Public Health," *Health Security*, Vol. 16, No. 3, 2018.

50 Disaster-related allostatic load can be detrimental to physical health (see Kazuomi Kario, Bruce S. McEwen, and Thomas G. Pickering, "Disasters and the Heart: A Review of the Effects of Earthquake-Induced Stress on Cardiovascular Disease," *Hypertension Research*, Vol. 26, No 5, 2003). There is also evidence that allostatic load can occur at community level (see Anita Chandra, Meagan Cahill, Douglas Yeung, and Rachel Ross, *Toward an Initial Conceptual Framework to Assess Community Allostatic Load: Early Themes from Literature Review and Community Analyses on the Role of Cumulative Community Stress*, Santa Monica, Calif.: RAND Corporation, RR-2559-RWJ, 2018).

51 For an overview of the role of differential vulnerability to disaster, see Shuhei Nomura, Alexander J. Q. Parsons, Mayo Hirabayashi, Ryo Kinoshita, Yi Liao, and Susan Hodgson, "Social Determinants of Mid-to Long-Term Disaster Impacts on Health: A

made continually over the course of the emergency, and ideally, lessons from previous responses and phases of the current response are considered and incorporated into plans for the next phase of the response as part of continual quality improvement and intra-action review processes.[52]

Eventually the health emergency transitions to recovery. Transition can occur because the impacts or projected impacts no longer warrant an emergency response, or—as can be the case for long-term health incidents—non-emergency systems have been established that can manage the incident in routine ways, meaning that incident management structures are no longer necessary (e.g., HIV/AIDS). This transition involves scaling down response, including disbanding part or all of the incident management structure, developing lessons learned and after-action reviews to improve future responses via PHEP and prevent public health hazards from spilling into disaster in the future, and supporting recovery of affected communities.

Summary

- Public health emergencies can occur with little to no warning depending on the causal triggering hazard. The early stages of an emergency, in particular, can involve confusion over the appropriate steps to take as experts grapple with understanding the emergency, specifically during novel disease outbreaks, such as the COVID-19 pandemic, when data do not exist to make informed decisions.
- Several features of public health emergencies make responses challenging. These include the many uncertainties surrounding the incident

Systematic Review," *International Journal of Disaster Risk Reduction*, Vol. 16, 2016. For a discussion on the need to modify communication to account for population differences in COVID, see Aaron Clark-Ginsberg and Elizabeth L. Petrun Sayers, "Communication Missteps During COVID-19 Hurt Those Already Most at Risk," *Journal of Contingencies and Crisis Management*, Vol. 28, No. 4, June 2020.

52 Margaret Chamberlin, Adeyemi Theophilus Okunogbe, Melinda Moore, and Mahshid Abir, *Intra-Action Report—A Dynamic Tool for Emergency Managers and Policymakers: A Proof of Concept and Illustrative Application to the 2014–2015 Ebola Crisis*, Santa Monica, Calif.: RAND Corporation, PE-147-RC, 2015.

itself and the large number of often-inexperienced stakeholders who respond to public health emergencies.
- Decisionmaking in response to a public health emergency can be complicated by uncertainty surrounding the nature of the incident. The scope and scale of a public health emergency are often unknown and difficult to predict at the outset, which can also complicate the decisionmaking on when to declare an emergency, mobilize resources, and prioritize where to apply those resources.

In the next section, we will discuss in greater detail the life cycle of significant cyber incidents. This will set up the cross-incident analysis in Chapter Four.

CHAPTER THREE

Life Cycle of Significant Cyber Incidents

A *cyber incident* is

> an event occurring on or conducted through a computer network that actually or imminently jeopardizes the integrity, confidentiality, or availability of computers, information or communications systems or networks, physical or virtual infrastructure controlled by computers or information systems, or information resident thereon.[1]

These types of incidents occur every day, and they are routinely addressed by regular coordination and response mechanisms. A *significant cyber incident* is a cyber incident that results in widespread disruption to critical lifeline sectors or NCFs[2] and in cascading impacts that affect national and homeland security, economic security, or public health and safety, including the possibility of injuries and deaths.

Significant cyber incidents, as we noted in the introduction, have been rare, and perhaps have not yet occurred in the United States. Even the 2020–2021 SolarWinds campaign did not significantly affect critical infrastructure or NCFs, although the scope of the intrusions was concerning enough

---

[1] White House, Office of the Press Secretary, 2016.

[2] *NCFs* are defined as

> [F]unctions of government and the private sector so vital to the United States that their disruption, corruption, or dysfunction would have a debilitating effect on security, national economic security, national public health or safety, or any combination thereof (CISA, undated-c).

for the federal government to convene a cyber UCG as part of the response.[3] However, we can learn from prior incidents, such as WannaCry[4] and the 2015 Ukraine electric grid attack,[5] which have demonstrated the potential for cyber incidents to rise to the level of a significant incident. Recalling the early history of the internet, the ARPANET-infecting Creeper worm of 1971 and the more-destructive Morris worm in 1988 (which reportedly infected 10 percent of all computers on the internet at that point) showed how systemic cyber effects can arise through self-replication and interconnectedness, even when there is no malicious intent motivating the precipitating event.[6] It is possible that error or unintended action may result in a significant cyber incident.

Because the next significant cyber incident will be unprecedented, we consider the potential decisionmaking challenges and how our responses might fail. Although this approach is necessarily speculative, the analysis is rooted in lessons from previous cyber incidents, including challenges revealed in those incidents, that remain yet unsolved. For instance, cyber effects may cause functional impacts that cannot be countered by IT responses alone; they may emanate from overseas infrastructure that the victims have no authority to intervene against; they may be part of a strategic campaign by an adaptive adversary that has already planned against the victims' likely initial responses; and they may trigger panic or active resis-

3 The UCG is envisioned as the primary response coordination body at the Federal level to convene relevant stakeholders and promote more integrated response to significant cyber incidents. White House, Office of the Press Secretary, 2016.

4 Lily Hay Newman, "How an Accidental 'Kill Switch' Slowed Friday's Massive Ransomware Attack," *Wired*, May 13, 2017.

5 A NATO researcher concluded that "[i]t seems likely that the more sophisticated and expensive NotPetya campaign is a declaration of power—demonstration of the acquired disruptive capability and readiness to use it" (see NATO Cooperative Cyber Defence Centre of Excellence, "NotPetya and WannaCry Call for a Joint Response from International Community," webpage, undated). Also, see SANS and Electricity Information Sharing and Analysis Center, *Analysis of the Cyber Attack on the Ukrainian Power Grid: Defense Use Case*, March 18, 2016; and Andy Greenberg, "The Untold Story of NotPetya, the Most Devastating Cyberattack in History," *Wired*, August 22, 2018.

6 Fred Kaplan, *Dark Territory: The Secret History of Cyber War*, New York: Simon & Schuster, 2016a, p. 60.

tance among the public. Anticipating the atypical characteristics of a significant cyber incident can inform a broader variety of potential responses, such as physical repairs, counterthreat operations, and efforts to combat disinformation. Anticipating the obstacles to effective decisionmaking can help avoid failed responses, such as delayed responses, incomplete participation in responses, and loss of confidence in responses.

Phases of a Significant Cyber Incident

A significant cyber incident can be understood in three simplified phases: pre-incident, the incident itself, and post-incident. The pre-incident phase includes some activities and events unique to that phase, such as adversarial and defensive preparations, and the potential emergence of indicators of intrusion or other anomalies. From the victim's perspective, the beginning of the incident itself may be difficult to determine, because the sequence of actions taken by an adversary is typically designed not to be obvious, and the resulting effects may be incremental. From the attacker's perspective, the beginning of the incident might be the moment the attacker takes non-reversible actions that are likely to draw attention, eventually, despite its efforts to evade detection.[7] Similarly, a precise transition to the post-incident phase is difficult to define because many infected devices, vulnerable systems, and impacts can persist even after the crisis response efforts have subsided. Additionally, some typical post-incident activities, such as forensic investigations, often also start during the initial stages of incident response.

Like other perpetrator-caused significant incidents, such as terrorism, significant cyber incident life cycles thus will be viewed differently, depending on the perspective from which they are viewed: from the adversary's perspective, the responder's perspective, and how the incident itself unfolds and can impact other systems and networks, which may not be readily apparent to the responder and even, at times, the attacker. Next, we describe

[7] We focus primarily on cyber incidents caused by a malicious actor as opposed to one caused by error or unintended action. The latter could theoretically also result in a significant cyber incident.

three perspectives (or characterizations) of a cyber incident life cycle that span the pre- through post-incident phases:

- attacker's perspective: stages that an adversary would follow to conduct an attack
- impact tracing: a series of events and consequences that emerge among interconnected and dependent systems
- responder's perspective: a progression of activities undertaken in response to a developing incident.

We can learn lessons for cyber incident response from each of these models. We explore them and the implications for response in the following section. In this section, we dwell in more detail on the different perspectives to analyze the nature of cyber incidents and response.

Stages of Attack: Cyber Kill Chain

Lockheed Martin's Cyber Kill Chain® is a familiar model to cybersecurity experts that describes the cyber incident life cycle from the perspective of the attacker and the steps that the adversary must take to achieve its objectives. The model describes the attack stages starting with reconnaissance and continuing through weaponization, delivery, exploitation, installation, command and control, and actions on objectives, as shown in Figure 3.1.

The Cyber Kill Chain model is helpful in understanding how an adversary develops a target and, ultimately, has an effect on the target, whether it is exfiltration of data or manipulation of system processes. It also helps a defender look for signals of adversary activity, particularly when paired with more detailed analysis of tactics, techniques, and procedures.[8] For example, for an adversary seeking to cause significant consequences through a cyber attack, reconnaissance may be broad-based across many systems and networks as the adversary develops a plan of attack and identifies vulnerabilities to exploit. There are also ongoing processes that either enable effects on a targeted system or achieve additional objectives not related to

[8] This is particularly helpful when paired with more-detailed analytic frameworks that build from the Cyber Kill Chain, such as the ATT&CK framework (see MITRE ATT&CK, homepage, undated).

FIGURE 3.1
Cyber Kill Chain®

SOURCE: Lockheed Martin, undated.

the target itself. These ongoing processes may provide an opportunity to disrupt the adversary's attack life cycle indirectly, or they may necessitate response efforts that address more than just the cyber effects themselves. For example, command and control and operational assessments are examples of ongoing effects-enabling activities, and disrupting them could help responders buy time to implement mitigations or to foil successive attacks. As another example, anti-forensics support the adversary's objectives of evading detection and culpability,[9] but preliminary attribution might provide enough technical and political leverage to coerce an adversary to halt an ongoing attack. Lastly, adversary strategic messaging is an ongoing process that can enhance impacts or enable qualitatively different impacts. This is especially true if the cyber operations are intended as a precursor to false attribution or inducing panic. Thus, counter-disinformation efforts could disrupt these later stages of the adversary's attack life cycle.

Series of Events and Consequences

Cyber incidents can also be viewed as a series of observable events and their consequences. Understanding these events and consequences can help identify some of the challenges responders will face and limitations of existing response plans.

Observable Events

Cyber incidents may include upstream events in red- (adversary cyberspace) and gray-space (neutral cyberspace), such as establishment of botnets and other infrastructure, insertion of payloads, and the seeding of command and control nodes and anti-forensics capabilities that will make victims' anticipated responses less effective. Many different stakeholders may collect or have data that are relevant to understanding these activities and their impacts. For example, government agencies may have insight into these activities through intelligence sources, while some private sector companies will have data from their own sources and infrastructure or through

---

[9] *Anti-forensics* are techniques to obscure or delete evidence of malicious activity to frustrate the investigation of a cyber incident (see Simson Garfinkel, "Anti-Forensics: Techniques, Detection and Countermeasures," 2nd International Conference on i-Warfare and Security, Monterey, Calif.: March 8–9, 2007).

aggregating information from cybersecurity monitoring services provided to their customers. In addition, cyber incidents involve anomalous activity on victim systems and resulting adverse events (e.g., unauthorized access, alteration of permissions or configurations, loss of control). The cyber effects may hijack, disable, or deny access to devices. One characteristic of these events is that emerging information about them primarily belongs to private sector owners and operators, who might not readily share it with other stakeholders. No single entity has access to all of this data, nor does any single entity have the responsibility and authority to integrate all of this data. This fracturing of data collection which may not be shared or fused effectively can result in limited warning or understanding of the scope of activity.

Cyber contagion entails the spreading of cyber effects across systems and networks. The mechanisms of contagion are not always obvious, yet the spread can be rapid across systems, networks, multiple sectors, and even continents. This presents a challenge in making accurate estimates of impact and in activating coordinated response plans prior to widespread infections.

Consequences

The functional impacts of a cyber incident can span degraded functionality of critical infrastructure, malfunctioning control systems, and operational or business disruptions. Responders might have difficulty in anticipating which systems may be affected, how the cyber effects may spread across systems, and which action will likely alleviate the functional impacts, especially if the underlying system is complex or difficult to model. This uncertainty may also affect stakeholders' decisions on whether and to what extent to invest in protective or resilience measures.

The secondary impacts of a cyber incident may include cascading impacts to other NCFs; panic or loss of confidence in systems or organizations; and other social, public health, economic, or national security impacts that were not directly targeted by the cyber effects. Poor decisionmaking early in a crisis, such as withholding information or assistance, can also undermine subsequent responses by, for instance, making other stakeholders less willing to coordinate and participate. In these cases, it is not the attack but the decisionmaking that can cause the secondary impacts.

Successive impacts can include recurrent cyber effects or functional impacts, potentially arising from pockets of unremediated IT systems, undetected active vectors, or uncoordinated recovery efforts. Successive impacts can also result from repeated or sustained attacks by the adversary or other malicious actors piggybacking on the attack. Flawed assessments can lead to wasted resources through premature remediation and recovery efforts.

Finally, even after the end of the proximate incident, the adversary may have persistent capabilities to cause an incident again. An adversary's cyberattack resources, infrastructure, and personnel will endure through the response to and recovery from a significant cyber incident unless the response involved *counterthreat operations* (which we define as either military, intelligence, or law enforcement actions to counter the threat actor either in neutral or adversary cyberspace). A continuing threat in adversary cyberspace suggests a full resolution to an adversarial significant cyber incident must also entail some form of deterrence or action to persuade the adversary not to use those capabilities again. Similarly, the end of the events life cycle also includes the likely persistence of data and hardware in friendly or neutral cyberspace. This refers to the continued availability of some elements of the affected information systems, which can be analyzed for forensic purposes and can inform future resilience measures based on what data and hardware could be recovered and how.

Identifying all the myriad ways a cyber incident can spread and affect other systems, sectors or NCFs are likely beyond the capacity of any group of planners, but it is possible to identify where an organization or group of organizations have strong dependent links to others and lead to subsequent pre-incident planning.[10] Often planners will want to understand the technical pathways that will lead to contagion of a cyber incident rather than focusing on the types of impacts to mitigate or prevent.

Understanding the wide variety of observable events and their consequences that may characterize a significant cyber attack suggests that most

[10] For more on this, see Steven M. Rinaldi, James P. Peerenboom, and Terrence K. Kelly, "Identifying, Understanding, and Analyzing Critical Infrastructure Interdependences," *IEEE Control Systems Magazine*, December 2001. The application of these concepts to planning is discussed in Kotila et al., forthcoming.

internal corporate cyber incident response playbooks may be inadequate as the foundation of response to a significant cyber incident, as they are intended to address only impacts to the company's own operations. A significant cyber incident by definition will affect economic security, public health, or national security. Thus, in a significant cyber incident, the actions of an affected entity could have profound implications for the functioning of an entire sector or national interests, or effects on adversary decisionmaking. These consequences are beyond the scope of most incident response playbooks, so an affected entity's responses, or the coordinated responses of others, depend on recognizing when events could result in broader consequences than just those affecting an individual entity.

Responder's Perspective: A Progression of Activities Undertaken in Response to a Developing Incident

A cyber incident can also be understood from the responder's perspective. Several federal and sector-specific guides describe response frameworks, although many of these are not designed for the scope, complexity, or severity of a significant cyber incident. Nevertheless, there is a significant amount of overlap in existing response frameworks, some of which address contagion, cross-sector impacts, the recurrence of effects and their consequences, and learning and adaptation. One of the few examples specifically designed for systemic, significant cyber incidents is the Financial Stability Board's Cyber Incident Response and Recovery Lifecycle. The overarching life cycle includes before, during, and after phases, and it further characterizes these into a progression of overlapping components: (1) governance, (2) planning and preparation, (3) analysis, (4) mitigation, (5) restoration and recovery, (6) coordination and communication, and (7) improvement.[11] These are shown in Figure 3.2.

One advantage of this framework is that it describes analysis and mitigation as concurrent activities that both support restoration and recovery. It also emphasizes the overlapping and cyclical nature of response and recovery. This means that responders should not think of incident response and recovery as a strictly linear process. There may be setbacks or other incidents that will require reassessing the severity and scope of the incident,

---

[11] Financial Stability Board, "Cyber Resilience," webpage, last updated January 6, 2021.

FIGURE 3.2
Cyber Incident Response and Recovery Life Cycle

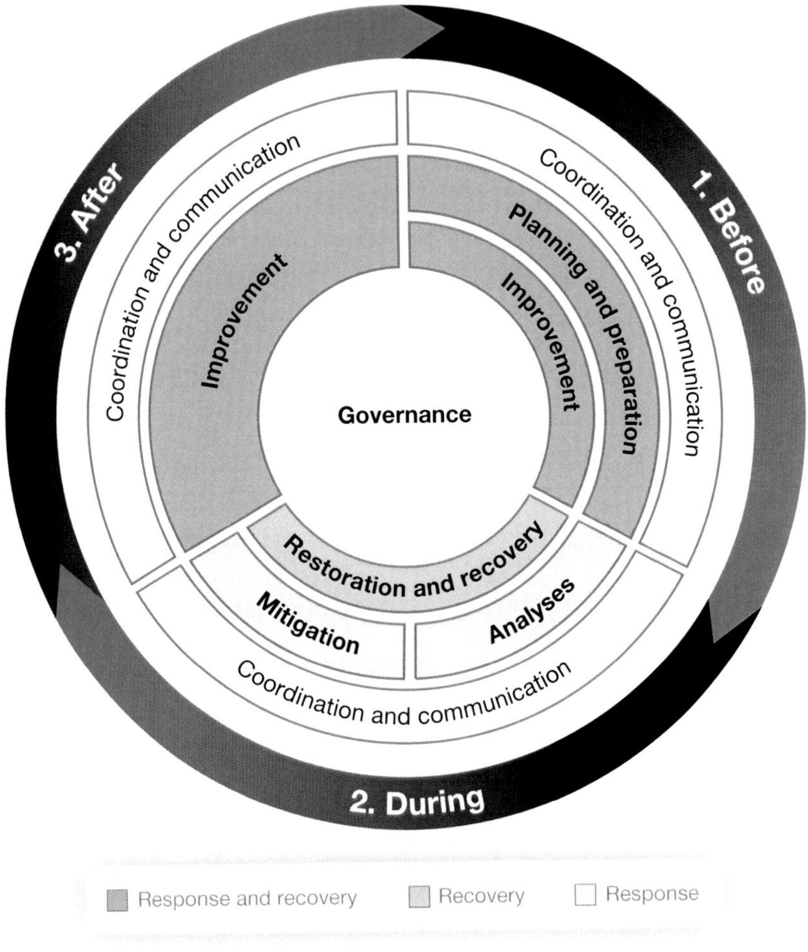

SOURCE: Financial Stability Board, last updated January 2021.

reallocation of resources, and notification and activation of response capabilities that may not have been initially mobilized.

In these cyber-specific frameworks, the subsequent stages depend on identifying the root cause, but this approach may be problematic in a significant cyber incident, which by definition is likely to cause severe impacts beyond the cyber domain and may be engineered by a sophisticated adversary to conceal the mechanisms of attack. Thus, a significant cyber incident may require parallel efforts to mitigate the downstream impacts while simultaneously working to identify and address the root cause. These two streams are important but have to be carefully managed to prevent dissipation of resources or even conflict between the two.

In a significant cyber incident, the ability to gather, collate, fuse, and analyze information may be challenged by the novel characteristics of the attack and the unprecedented scale, scope, or severity of the impacts. Thus, it may be the case that responders will be operating without the level of situational awareness that they are accustomed to in more typical cyber incidents. Because of the speed of cyber effects and their downstream impacts, and the resulting narrow windows of opportunity, responders will likely have to make decisions under conditions of great uncertainty. If decision-makers wait too long to gather more details about the threat, they might miss opportunities to contain the cyber effects by isolating networks or taking systems offline, or to mitigate the downstream impacts through notifications to apply protections or find alternatives. On the other hand, there is also risk to committing resources and to actions early in an incident.

Impacts of Significant Cyber Incidents

As noted earlier, the U.S. government's definition of a significant cyber incident is broad and could encompass many different impacts across NCFs and sectors ("demonstrable harm to the national security interests, foreign relations, or economy of the United States or to the public confidence, civil liberties, or public health and safety of the American people"). A significant cyber incident or series of incidents could have far-reaching impacts across many sectors and functions, resulting potentially in disruption to critical lifeline functions (e.g., transportation, water, energy, and communication) that have subsequent physical impacts, such as injury and loss of life. The combination of cyber impacts that disrupt systems and networks and the subsequent physical impacts will require response to address both types of impacts, as we noted above in the discussion of consequences.

Initial Assessment and Determination of a Significant Cyber Incident Can Be Difficult to Achieve

One of the core challenges in a cyber attack is that response options and decision timelines are shaped, in part, by the adversary. The next subsection will address this dynamic—but, first, we examine determinations and decision points that might arise in a significant cyber incident, and how they might be problematic regardless of an adversary's actions.

Determining when a response is needed is not straightforward. In the absence of early warning, the speed or subtlety of cyber effects means that, from the victim's perspective, observed impacts will tend to precede the identification of root causes. Thus, an initial response would be prompted by the emergence of adverse events or even serious consequences. In this case, responders would be managing both functional and cyber effects in parallel, and potentially having to decide which effort to prioritize. However, the reverse is possible, where a suspected threat is identified prior to the effects taking hold, and monitored as it develops from an adverse event on an information system into an operational disruption. Although this decision path provides more opportunities for protection and containment, it is highly dependent on prior foundational determinations. These include (1) distinguishing a typical cyber threat from a serious one and also pre-threat determinations of which systems to monitor in the first place and (2) investing in relevant detection and response capabilities.

When to alert others about the threat is a key decision point. The federal government, private sector partners, and customers might all benefit from some degree of advance notice of an emerging threat. But private sector entities may be reluctant to admit that their systems were compromised, if they are aware of the compromise at all, and there is also the risk of desensitizing responders by reacting too often to indicators or to false positive alerts. The federal government may be reluctant to share sensitive intelligence at a level of detail that is actionable, although the number of cleared personnel in various sectors has increased in recent years.[12] The creation of interagency, cross-sector watch floors for critical infrastructure and cyber

[12] Department of Homeland Security, "DHS/CISA/PIA – 020 Private Sector Clearance Program for Critical Infrastructure," webpage, last updated November 12, 2021.

incidents could support timely notification. Yet sharing timely information about these threats also depends on recognizing their seriousness and potential significance to others.

Assessing the seriousness or severity of a threat is a critical activity in incident response, especially given the volume of malicious activity and the qualitatively different response that significant cyber incidents are supposed to entail; specifically, a whole-of-nation response that cannot be summoned for repeated false alarms. Thus, a key determination is the severity of the impacts, including assessing the potential for cascading effects and successive impacts. Underestimating these factors could result in delays in activating coordinated response plans and in missed opportunities to contain the threat or to proactively apply protection and mitigation measures. In addition to the challenge of making accurate predictions of impacts, another problem lies in various stakeholders using different standards to evaluate the severity of threats. This includes not just the estimates themselves but the level of confidence in those estimates. Although the National Cyber Incident Severity System is available for use by all sectors and critical infrastructure operators, many have their own internal processes and tailored criteria, which could lead to different assessments of the severity of an emerging incident.[13] The Office of the Director of National Intelligence (ODNI)'s Cyber Threat Intelligence Integration Center may attempt to consolidate and rationalize these assessments to provide a consensus view of the incident's severity.[14]

Notification and assessments are related to, but distinct from, activating coordinated response plans. Escalating the response posture beyond internal playbooks could be a challenging process because an additional degree of cooperation is required. For instance, even if sector and federal entities are in communication, the affected entity may be reluctant to involve the other in its response, or the sector and federal government may not agree the threshold has been met for a broader response. A potential hazard here is waiting for internal playbooks to be proven inadequate before requesting or providing external assistance. PPD-41 provides mechanisms to facili-

---

13 CISA, "CISA National Cyber Incident Scoring System," webpage, undated-a.

14 ODNI, "Cyber Threat Framework," webpage, undated-a; ODNI, "Cyber Threat Intelligence Integration Center," webpage, undated-b.

tate consensus-building and to mobilize a unified response in the form of the Cyber UCG and the Cyber Response Group.[15] Additionally, if a cyber incident is precipitated by a sophisticated nation state actor, we can also expect that actor to interfere with incident responders' ability to communicate effectively with each other, such as through targeting communications networks and links. These actors may also execute additional cyber attacks against other systems that support response to the physical impacts of an incident, such as interfering with emergency response deployment or hospital systems.

Adversaries Can Influence Decisions and Available Response Options

One challenge cyber incident responders should expect in a significant cyber incident is that an adversary (if there is one causing the incident) likely has crafted its attack to limit the number of response options available. Also, it may have planned a series of attacks as part of a sustained campaign, not just one attack. Decisionmakers may face a dearth of relevant response capabilities, narrow windows of opportunity to use certain response options, or resource constraints for recovering from impacts. They also may have to consider how to allocate resources when the full scope of an incident or series of incidents is potentially unclear at the outset when faced with a sophisticated adversary. However, workarounds and alternatives may provide temporary functionality until the cyber effects, such as data loss and disabled hardware, can be reversed. For example, Maersk experienced only a 20-percent drop in shipping volume during the NotPetya incident because of "human resilience," such as manual workarounds and the cooperation of customers,[16] despite having to replace or restore 4,000 servers, 45,000 PCs, and 2,500 applications. Additionally, Maersk's fast recovery was attributed, in part, to its multi-channel, fact-based, leadership-driven public communications and internal coordination.[17]

---

15 White House, Office of the Press Secretary, 2016.

16 World Economic Forum, "Securing a Common Future in Cyberspace," video, January 24, 2018.

17 Luck may have also played a role. Maersk reportedly was able to replicate its domain controllers (servers used to authenticate users on a network) from a remote office that

The 2015 attack on Ukraine's power grid exemplifies how a well-prepared and coordinated attack plan can confound responses, but also how workarounds and alternatives can mitigate the impacts. According to a report by Electricity Information Sharing Analysis Center, "the strongest capability of the attackers was not in their choice of tools or in their expertise, but in their capability to perform long-term reconnaissance operations required to learn the environment and execute a highly synchronized, multistage, multisite attack."[18] The attackers' extensive reconnaissance and infiltration enabled access to multiple critical systems, allowing them to combine an array of attack mechanisms. First, they reconfigured the uninterruptable power supply to go down when the grid attack occurred, so that the operators would also be in the dark. Second, they installed malicious firmware at the substations so operators would not be able to send remote commands to reset the breakers. Third, they hijacked user accounts and their terminals so the attackers could act as the operators and open the breakers themselves. Fourth, they executed a telephone denial-of-service attack to flood power companies' call centers with fake calls so real customers could not report outages. These tactics bought some time for the attackers to synchronize opening the breakers at numerous substations belonging to multiple power companies. However, some experts say the telephone denial-of-service attack had another goal: "to stoke the ire of Ukrainian customers and weaken their trust in the Ukrainian power companies and government."[19] Loss of confidence is a possible outcome of flawed or, in this case, constrained decision-making. In the end, Ukrainian power companies were able to restore service over the course of several days only because the substations had manual controls that offered an alternative to using the remote commands.[20]

Figure 3.3 provides examples of determinations and decision points that might arise in a significant cyber incident. Some of these would also arise in more typical cyber incidents, such as identifying adverse events and activating internal response playbooks, whereas others would be more char-

happened to be down during the NotPetya attack (see Greenberg, 2020, p. 194).

[18] SANS and Electricity Information Sharing and Analysis Center, 2016.

[19] Greenberg, 2018.

[20] SANS and Electricity Information Sharing and Analysis Center, 2016.

FIGURE 3.3

Examples of Decision Points for Cyber Incident Response

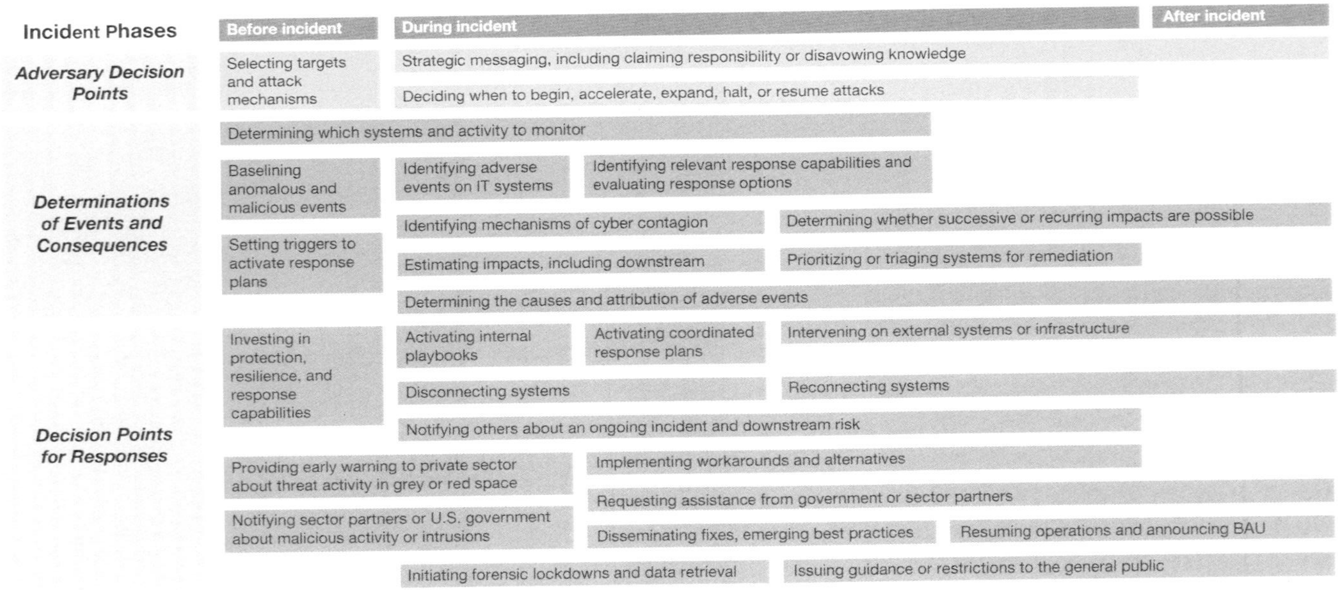

SOURCES: RAND analysis of the aforementioned cyber incidents and the following documents: Michael Bartock, Jeffrey Cichonski, Murugiah Souppaya, Matthew Smith, Gregory Witte, and Karen Scarfone, *Guide for Cybersecurity Event Recovery*, Gaithersburg, Md.: National Institute of Standards and Technology, SP 800-184, December 2016; CISA, undated-a; Financial Stability Board, *Effective Practices for Cyber Incident Response and Recovery: Final Report*, Basel, Switzerland, October 19, 2020; and National Infrastructure Advisory Council, *Actionable Cyber Intelligence: An Executive-Led Collaborative Model*, Washington, D.C., December 2020.

NOTE: BAU = business as usual.

acteristic of significant cyber incidents. These include adversary decision points such as halting or resuming attacks, or engaging in strategic messaging alongside the cyber attack itself. These also may include determinations such as which systems to triage or prioritize for remediation, and decisions to intervene on systems that are not owned or operated by the affected entities or the U.S. government. The figure shows determinations and decision points occurring before, during, and after the incident, but it also shows some of these spanning multiple phases. For instance, determining the causes and attribution of adverse events occurs both during and after the incident, because it supports forensics, IT solutions, and potentially counter-adversary activities, all of which might also continue after the immediate impacts of the incident are resolved. The figure also shows determinations and decisions that overlap with some but not others. For example, a decision to disconnect systems or take them offline, which would be a protective or containment measure, generally would come before determinations about which systems to prioritize for remediation, because that is a recovery and restoration measure. As another example, disseminating fixes and best practices should come before a decision to reconnect systems that had been taken offline. These decisions and determinations are mutually interdependent and may differ based on the specific incident, so the timelines represented here are merely notional; however, they do suggest when the windows of opportunity for certain activities might close and which determinations might be required prior to moving on to other response options.

Figure 3.4 considers how various anticipated characteristics of a significant cyber incident could confound decisionmaking and lead to negative outcomes. This figure reflects how it is not just the targets or attack mechanism but also the challenges in the decisionmaking environment that can precipitate or exacerbate some impacts. The first column describes several plausible or anticipated features of organizations, capabilities, information, and cyber effects that might help characterize the incident environment and response posture that is inherited at the beginning of a significant cyber incident. The example in the first row is of various stakeholders using different assessment methodologies and standards to make determinations of such things as incident severity or the urgency of response. These characteristics are meant to be neutral in the sense that they do not pose a hazard

FIGURE 3.4

Potential Paths to Cyber Incident Response Failures

Anticipated characteristics of a significant cyber incident	Potential response hazards	Effects on decision points (1 of 2)	Negative consequences or outcomes (1 of 2)	Effects on decision points (2 of 2)	Negative consequences or outcomes (2 of 2)
Stakeholders have different assessment standards and methodologies	Cannot agree that thresholds for responses have been met	Activating coordinated response plans is delayed	Public messaging is uncoordinated and conflicting	Requests for assistance from U.S. government or sector partners are denied, delayed	Effects worsen until secondary or successive impacts prompt responses
Uncertainty over which devices will be affected	Not enough replacement devices are stockpiled	Difficulty identifying relevant response capabilities	Restoration efforts are slowed by supply chain	Prioritization and triage become contentious	Competition among affected entities inhibits coordinated response
Early warning information primarily belongs to government.	Sensitive intelligence is not shared with private sector	Determining what systems to monitor is not informed by intelligence	Loss of trust in U.S. government and the coordinated response plan	Adverse events occur without the context of seriousness or intent	Effects spread and gain persistence; missed opportunities for protection and containment
Information on critical infrastructure adverse events primarily belongs to private sector	Firms fail to share potentially embarrassing or compromising info with competitors and the U.S. government	Notification of potential downstream impacts does not occur	Secondary impacts occur before protections or mitigations are put in place	Identification of adverse events, causes, mechanisms of contagion is uninformed and uncoordinated	Unnecessarily severe impacts; loss of trust in firms
Affected entity response typically should be handled by sector	Requests for U.S. government assistance granted only after internal playbooks fail	Response options are sought to substitute for the withheld USG capabilities	Affected entities conduct "hack back" operations, escalate conflict	Delayed activation of coordinated response plans	Worsening impacts and loss of trust
Cyber effects may utilize third-party infrastructure	Third-parties are not consulted about responses	Response options are misinformed	Unanticipated downstream impacts from interventions	Inaccurate public messaging and failures to notify	Loss of confidence in U.S. government and the coordinated response plan
Private sector has little visibility into gray- and red-space activities	Private sector firms develop playbooks based only on their own operations	Determining what systems to monitor is not informed by adversary activities	Impacts worsen while trying to gain situational awareness	Reconnecting systems is not informed by adversary activities	Repeated attacks and persistent threats reverse the recovery
Cyber effects may be emanating from overseas, foreign-owned systems	Authorities to intervene overseas are limited and reserved for U.S. government	Interventions on overseas systems are delayed by political considerations	Impacts worsen and conflict widens	Difficulty determining root causes and attack attribution	Loss of trust and confidence in foreign nations; possible false flag
Persistence of uninoculated systems, including upstream connected nodes	Compliance with directives is unknown, and possibly incomplete or resisted	Resuming operations is not informed by the likelihood of successive impacts	Reinfections reverse the recovery and deplete hardware reserves	Public communications escalate from guidance to restrictions to enforcement	Loss of trust among general public and affected entities

by themselves, and they may even be advantageous in other circumstances; however, there are potential hazards closely associated with these characteristics in the context of an emerging significant cyber incident. The second column provides an example of these hazards from which the other columns will later extrapolate, creating the "paths to response failures." These hazards may take the form of, for example, a lack of preparation, a failure to coordinate, or an irreversible decision, all of which are hazards in the sense that they can confound subsequent decisions and cause negative consequences. The example in the first row is that the stakeholders cannot agree that certain response thresholds have been met because they are using different assessment methodologies and standards. The third column extrapolates from this hazard how it might affect a subsequent determination or decision point (of the kind listed in Figure 3.3). Generally, the effect is to delay, misinform, or otherwise confound decisionmaking. The example in the first row is a delay in deciding to activate a coordinated response plan because some stakeholders believe the threshold has not yet been met. The fourth column describes negative consequences or outcomes that might result from these confounded determinations or decision points. Thus, the fourth column should encapsulate a response failure, whereby the response itself exacerbates the impacts, or creates additional problems beyond what the cyber effects themselves are causing. The fifth and sixth columns play the same role as the third and fourth columns, respectively, simply providing a second pair of effects and consequences.

Each step in these paths from characteristics to consequences is notional, but they are meant to capture decisionmaking challenges that might arise in a significant cyber incident to consider solutions, such as preparation and resilience measures, that can be agreed on and implemented ahead of time.

What aspects of a significant cyber incident will challenge the decisionmakers, and how will that potentially reduce the effectiveness of our responses? Potential paths to response failures are described in Figure 3.4.

Summary

Responding to significant cyber incidents bears some similarities with other types of incident response as we have highlighted in prior sections. The particular challenges in cyber incident response, however, include the significant scope of uncertainty in the early stages of an incident surrounding the likely scale and severity, and how the incident may evolve as impacts spread across systems and networks. This challenge is not unique to cyber incidents but has potentially a much greater spectrum of uncertainty compared with a natural hazard or a terrorist incident.

The various stakeholders to an incident response may have vastly different views on severity and impact, which will impact the degree to which they may coordinate their response activities across government and private sector response activities. Cyber incident response as articulated in the NCIRP places great responsibility for response on the private sector, supported by government agencies in supporting roles, which is also a distinguishing feature compared with emergency responses to natural hazards, public health emergencies, or terrorist incidents.

Emergency management to natural hazards has a long history of lessons learned and evolved processes that support better coordination (despite some continued weaknesses), whereas cyber incident response at the scale of a significant incident does not have this history and experience from which to build.

In the following chapter, we will provide a more detailed comparison across incident types.

CHAPTER FOUR

Cross-Incident Analysis

In the previous two chapters, we provided overviews of each incident type, the response to the incident, and key decisions that inform the response. In this section, we synthesize this analysis by identifying similarities and differences between the incident types, with particular attention on how they might affect incident response. There may be multiple ways in which incidents can be compared, but not all those comparisons will bear on incident response.

Incident Origins, Identification, and Attribution May Consume Cyber Incident Response Resources

There are several distinctions between the origins and how responders first identify an incident that can affect decisionmaking. Some natural hazards, such as hurricanes, can provide warning that allows for pre-staging of response capabilities and assessment of severity to inform mobilization of resources. A significant cyber incident, on the other hand, is less likely to reveal its full scope immediately and can, as we saw with the NotPetya case, have unintended knock-on impacts in other sectors and systems. In terrorist incidents there is also uncertainty over the scope and scale of an attack which may include multiple targets, but in most cases, we can expect those to be limited.

In both cyber and terrorist incidents, attribution of the incident can consume considerable time and resources, and impacts how responders think about the incident. Many of the first responders—whether they be fire and medical teams in the case of a terror attack or incident response teams for cyber—will want to focus their attention on addressing the most pressing and immediate impacts of the incident, but for cyber and terror incidents there is also a focus on determining who is responsible to determine whether to expect additional impacts or additional attacks. Cyber and terror incidents will involve other stakeholders, such as federal law enforcement and the Intelligence Community, that would not ordinarily be expected for natural hazards.

Who Responds Differs Across Incident Types; Cyber Incident Response Will Be Led by Private Sector–Affected Entities

The key players in response activities will vary across the incident types for several reasons, which will also affect decisionmaking in response. For natural hazards, local officials and first responders are typically the first to identify and mobilize to respond. However, as the scope and scale of a natural hazard grow, the state or states affected will mobilize resources, including through the activation of mutual assistance mechanisms. (Federal resources can be brought to bear through an emergency or disaster declaration.) Because there is no adversary as such to respond to, the focus of attention is on saving lives and restoring essential services, before transitioning to long-term recovery. Occasionally, natural hazards will overlap, such as when Hurricanes Irma and Maria hit Puerto Rico in rapid succession, or hazards will occur concurrently, such as large-scale wildfires in the Western United States in recent years.[1] Such conditions will place additional strains on responders and lead to fractured attention—however, overall, the lines of authority and the primary responsibility for coordinating response are clearly laid out and understood. Terror incidents will involve local responders but will also trigger federal involvement, primarily in from law enforcement. Responding to cyber incidents, however, is seen in federal policies and response frameworks as first and foremost the responsibility of the affected entities, whether they are large corporations, school districts, or

1 RAND Corporation, "Hurricanes Irma and Maria: Impact and Aftermath," webpage, undated

health care systems. This is not to say that state and federal authorities do not play a role in assisting with response, but it is usually based on an assistance request from the affected entity and may not be timely. In a significant cyber incident that is affecting multiple entities and sectors, early response can see many different actors making decisions independently. The system of response for cyber incidents leans on those developed for natural hazards as we noted earlier, but they are less well practiced for cyber incidents and introduce new decisionmaking bodies such as the cyber UCG.

At the federal level, FEMA leads response to natural hazards, and other agencies, including the Department of Defense, play supporting roles. In terror incidents, the FBI is the lead for coordinating the federal response and investigating the incident.[2] For cyber incidents, the responsibility at the federal level is divided by policy between the FBI (lead for threat response) and Department of Homeland Security (lead for asset response), with support from others in the U.S. government, including the Intelligence Community and the Department of Defense as appropriate. Within the Department of Defense, there is an additional division of responsibilities in which U.S. Northern Command has the lead for support to civil authorities and homeland defense, while U.S. Cyber Command has the capabilities and capacity to provide defense support to cyber incident response.[3]

At the state level and in some municipalities, there are integrated emergency management or homeland security offices that are integrating capabilities and responsibility for cyber and other forms of incident response. Examples include the California Office of Emergency Services and the Texas Department of Public Safety. Many states are integrating cyber incident planning and capabilities into their centralized emergency services.

---

2 FBI, "What Is the FBI's Role in Combating Terrorism?" webpage, undated-c.

3 Cyber support is governed by Directive-Type Memorandum (DTM) 17-007, "Interim Policy and Guidance for Defense Support to Cyber Incident Response," U.S. Department of Defense, June 21, 2017. The DTM has been extended multiple times with the intent of replacing it with a Department of Defense directive at some future date.

Decisionmaking Is Often More Complex in Cyber Incidents

The types of decisions required in responding to a cyber incident do not vary in type from other incidents but are potentially far more complex due to the uncertainties and confusion that can shape the decisionmaking environment compared with other circumstances. Natural hazards can be unpredictable in several respects, such as when shifts in winds cause a change in the intensity and direction of a wildfire, or the changes in the scale of a hurricane, but these are known variables that responders can plan for in advance. Terror attacks also involve uncertainty, particularly in the early stages when responders need to assess whether to expect further attacks and, in the case of biological or chemical agents, understanding the nature of the attacks. Public health emergencies are often characterized by uncertainty and confusion in the early stages as well. However, it appears that cyber incidents have a much broader set of uncertainties to contend with, including the potential for significantly greater scaling of attacks and that an adversary can choose to attack many different targets as response gets underway. Assessing the severity of a cyber incident is difficult to do in the early stages of an incident where the number of affected systems will be unknown and the potential for cascading effects is broad. Impacted entities may not know immediately that they have been affected, though the nature of a *significant* cyber incident is such that it should become apparent at least in terms of impacts if not in terms of cause.

Transition points in cyber incident response are also difficult to discern with accuracy. The assessment of the incident will continue throughout the response as new information comes to light, and responders will have to make decisions under great uncertainty about how and when to transition resources from immediate response to mitigation and recovery.

In Table 4.1, we summarize some of the key aspects of the incident types we have analyzed here to highlight the distinctions and similarities across incident types that bear on response. The ratings of *high*, *moderate*, or *low* are relative ratings to indicate the distinctions between the types of incidents and are not scaled to specific measures. The table is derived from an examination of a limited number of prior incidents of each type and reflects contingent analysis of some of the ways that each of the incident types differ

TABLE 4.1

Comparison of Incident Types

Incident Type	Warning of Incident?	Degree of Uncertainty in Early Incident Stages	Level of Responder Experience	Diversity of Responder Communities
Terror Attacks	Sometimes	High	High	Moderate
Natural Hazards	Sometimes	Moderate	High	Moderate
Public Health Emergencies	Sometimes	Moderate to High	Moderate to High	High
Significant Cyber Incidents	Rare	High	Low to Moderate	High

in how they are relevant to decisionmaking in incident response. It is possible that examination of a larger number of incidents of each type could yield different characterizations.

The table illustrates that, compared with terror attacks, natural hazards, and public health emergencies, significant cyber incidents are likely to have fewer warnings, may be characterized by higher degrees of uncertainty, lower levels of responder experience, and a greater diversity of responder communities. Collectively, these factors may make responding to a significant cyber incident more challenging: limited warning makes early intervention difficult; high early stage uncertainty can make initial interventions difficult to calibrate correctly and can limit effectiveness; with less experience, responders may not be able to respond as quickly or effectively; and a greater diversity of responder communities may find it more difficult to coordinate and agree on appropriate response actions as the incident unfolds. These characterizations, of course, would not necessarily apply in all cases and are not determinative.

Implications for Cyber Incident Response

The implications of foregoing improving cyber incident response point to the limitations of applying systems and processes from other incident types. Response to natural hazards is built on decades of operational experience in the roles, responsibilities, available resources, processes, and required capabilities, although these systems are being stretched by the increasing severity and frequency of large-scale incidents.[4] Terrorist incidents, particularly in the United States and Western Europe, are much less frequent, but they still have established mechanisms for response. Public health emergencies can be localized or global in nature, and there can be significant uncertainty around the severity and speed with which a localized event can spread, as the ongoing global COVID-19 pandemic indicates. This could mean that coordination across stakeholders could be complicated because of differing assessments of the severity or potential for a localized public health emergency to spread, a similar set of conditions that would apply in cyber incident response. Despite efforts to establish frameworks and processes for cyber incident response that can rise to the level of a significant incident, the lack of experience in exercising those mechanisms in a robust manner means that we do not know how robust those mechanisms will support an effective response.

In addition to tested response procedures, resourcing response to any type of incident is also a critical consideration. Response to natural hazards falls first on the local and state governments responding, but a major disaster or emergency declaration can mobilize additional resources particularly through the Stafford Act. The Stafford Act can also provide resources in cases of terrorism, which occurred in 1995 after the Oklahoma City bombing, in response to the 9/11 terror attacks, and after the 2013 Boston Marathon bombings.[5] Currently the Stafford Act does not extend to cyber incidents, though some have called for the law to be amended to include cyber

4 Deanne Criswell, "FEMA Administrator Deanne Criswell's Remarks to the 2021 IAEM Conference," webpage, October 18, 2021; and Mike Ives, "California's Fires Are Stretching Crews and Stranding Evacuees," *New York Times*, August 20, 2021.

5 Bruce R. Lindsay, *Stafford Act Assistance and Acts of Terrorism*, Washington, D.C.: Congressional Research Service, R44801, last updated January 16, 2019.

incidents and pandemics.[6] Cyber incidents can only qualify for the Stafford Act if subsequent impacts from the incident caused a coverable event, such as an explosion.

Perhaps most significant to understand is how the various stakeholders will work together to detect and analyze an emerging cyber incident, agree on what forms of response are needed, and coordinate their activities to achieve mutually desired outcomes. As we noted earlier, some affected entities may not wish to share information on an incident, whether because of concerns over legal liabilities or reputational impact, or because they simply do not yet understand the full scope of the incident. In the aftermath of major ransomware events affecting such companies as Colonial Pipeline and JBS (a meat processing conglomerate) in 2021, Congress passed legislation mandating reporting to federal authorities—and CISA, in particular—within 72 hours.[7] But these proposals would only cover reporting of an incident. The type of information that would be reported is still under debate, and how CISA might be able to act on that information is also unclear because it has no legal authority to impose its response capabilities on an affected entity or entities.

The disparities in response capabilities are also a consideration for cyber incidents. Organizations of all types have been affected by cyber attacks in recent years, from hospitals and local governments to major international oil and gas companies and manufacturers. Larger companies and organizations tend to have greater internal capacity to respond to cyber incidents or may have contingency contracts with cybersecurity firms, while smaller companies, local governments, and others will have far less response capacity. That said, the response capacity that exists is largely geared toward addressing incidents below the threshold of the significant cyber incidents we have covered in this report, and different sectors have vastly different capabilities to respond both at an individual and a sector level. Even those companies that have developed robust incident response plans do not usu-

---

[6] Mark Gerencser, Alex Gorsky, and Jeh C. Johnson, *Findings and Recommendations of the BENS Commission on the National Response Enterprise: A Call to Action*, Washington, D.C.: Business Executives for National Security, February 2021.

[7] See, for example, Jonathan Reed, "U.S. Congress Approves Strengthening American Cybersecurity Act," *Security Intelligence*, March 30, 2022.

ally anticipate or plan for cyber incidents that would impact their entire organization, including back-up systems such as back-up data storage systems.[8] At the same time, the federal government has substantial cyber capabilities, resident in CISA, the FBI, the intelligence community (particularly NSA but others, too), and the Department of Defense. Coordinating these capabilities and planning for supporting incident response has been a focus for more than a decade now, dating at least as far back as 2010 when the Department of Homeland Security and Department of Defense signed a memorandum of agreement on cyber cooperation, but as the Department of Defense Inspector General and the Cyberspace Solarium Commission have noted, deficiencies in implementing these coordinating activities remain.[9]

The foregoing analysis indicates that a significant cyber incident can and should leverage lessons learned from other types of incidents, but those insights can only be taken so far. A significant cyber incident will likely require many different stakeholders to respond effectively, potentially a more diverse set than almost any other type of incident. The physical impacts of a significant cyber incident will draw on the mechanisms established for other forms of emergency management but will still require making several critical decisions early in an incident when the degree of uncertainty is high. In the next chapter we discuss steps to prepare better for significant cyber incidents.

---

8 Greenberg, 2020, pp. 193–195.

9 Department of Defense, Office of Inspector General, *Audit of the Department of Defense's Implementation of the Memorandums Between the Department of Defense and the Department of Homeland Security Regarding Cybersecurity and Cyberspace Operations*, Washington, D.C., DODIG-2021-100, July 13, 2021; and King and Gallagher, 2020.

CHAPTER FIVE

Recommendations and Areas for Future Research

Our analysis indicates that significant cyber incident response is distinct from other types of response that we examined and, therefore, requires additional work to set up the United States for effective response in the future. In this chapter, we provide some recommendations for taking steps to improve response, and highlight areas where further research is needed.

Recommendations

Improving Exercises to Address Critical Uncertainties in Response Planning and Execution

The United States may well find itself facing a significant cyber incident and lacking the fundamental building blocks of a coordinated response across public and private sector entities. The U.S. government and many private sector organizations have recognized the need to improve the coordination and planning for cyber incident response. The Cyberspace Solarium Commission recommended and Congress passed into law several provisions to spur this planning. Congress mandated the creation of a Joint Cyber Planning Office and a new national cyber exercise series in the fiscal year 2021 National Defense Authorization Act.[1] The new exercise series comes on top

[1] Sections 1715 and 1744, respectively, of the fiscal year 2021 National Defense Authorization Act (see Public Law 116-283, William M. [Mac] Thornberry National Defense Authorization Act for Fiscal Year 2021, January 1, 2021).

of existing national exercises, such CISA's Cyber Storm,[2] FEMA's National Level Exercise,[3] and the North American Electric Reliability Corporation's GridEx.[4] These exercises, joint planning efforts, and forthcoming guidance from CISA on cyber incident contingency planning are all welcome efforts. However, the National Level Exercises often lack the dynamic play and injects that can test critical assumptions and force participants to grapple with the issues we have identified here.[5] Large-scale exercises of these types with hundreds of participants are difficult to orchestrate and to facilitate for such dynamic play to occur. Participants we have spoken with in some of these exercises have lamented the scripted format and felt that the exercises did not allow them to understand the operational and tactical impacts of the decisions they had to make.

However, it may be too much to expect such large exercises to address these questions on their own. Rather than attempting to address all the various aspects of cyber incident response in an exercise, CISA and others should consider developing a series of exercises that focus on the different challenges we have identified here in turn. The series would first examine incident identification and assessment, followed by a focus on when and how to declare a significant cyber incident and mobilize resources, and conclude with scenarios that test transition points. Of course, asking participants to identify a significant cyber incident can appear artificial for an exercise explicitly designed to address this question, in which case the exercise planners could play multiple scenarios, not all of which result in a significant cyber incident. The purpose is not to trick the participants but to highlight the uncertainties, identify critical information requirements, and spur follow-on action, such as establishing information-sharing requirements and protections.

---

2 CISA, "Cyber Storm: Securing Cyber Space," webpage, undated-b.

3 FEMA, "National Level Exercise," webpage, updated July 21, 2020b; and FEMA, "National Level Exercise 2020," webpage, July 23, 2020c. The COVID-19 pandemic led the FEMA administrator to cancel most of the remaining events planned for the National Level Exercise in 2020.

4 North American Electric Reliability Corporation, "GridEx," webpage, undated.

5 Discussions with exercise participants. These views may not reflect the views of all the exercise participants.

Conducting Analysis to Inform Incident Identification

The first step in responding to a significant cyber incident is to know when it is occurring, as we have noted previously. Because the vectors that can lead to a standard cyber incident and a significant cyber incident are often similar, and often occur well in advance of the incident's discovery or effects manifest, differentiating between the two in the early stages is a challenge. That said, early detection in either case increases the chances of preventing or containing cyber contagion and is in itself a desirable goal. In the potentially more likely circumstances in which the initial stages are not detected until it is too late, organizations would benefit from having a clearer understanding of the potential grave impacts of a cyber incident—the secondary and tertiary effects that often lead to the most significant consequences. This understanding involves analysis of the ways in which complex systems could fail and lead to cascading effects so that cyber incident responders and other entities can establish indicators to watch out for. The National Labs have conducted similar analyses, particularly for the energy sector, and developed methods that also can inform this planning.[6]

Determining When a Significant Cyber Incident Has Occurred and Warrants Activating Joint Public-Private Incident Response Plans

The NCIRP states that a "Cyber UCG will be formed and activated only in the event of a significant cyber incident" and provides several mechanisms for convening the Cyber UCG, but it is unclear who ultimately makes the determination that a significant cyber incident is occurring.[7] In past work we have done in support of the Department of Homeland Security, including facilitating a cyber incident tabletop exercise involving federal government stakeholders and representatives from the private sector, we have observed

6 See, for example, Idaho National Laboratory, "Consequence-Driven Cyber-Informed Engineering," webpage, undated and Sandia National Laboratory, "IDART: Information Design Assurance Red Team," webpage, undated. These methods are primarily intended to inform vulnerability identification and secure engineering, but they could also be used to tabletop consequences.

7 Department of Homeland Security, 2016.

that the U.S. government and the private sector may not agree when a significant cyber incident is emerging; private sector organizations may wish to delay a determination until more information is gathered and analyzed, while the federal government may be more inclined to make that determination earlier. The declaration of a significant cyber incident does not automatically trigger any particular response, and it currently does not confer any additional authority, such as allowing the federal government to intervene to respond domestically. Domestic cyber incident response still largely depends on voluntary coordination and cooperation between the public and private sectors.

CISA has identified this as an area requiring additional work, and one in which joint public-private contingency planning could help identify required information and agreed mechanisms for such a declaration. The Homeland Security Operational Analysis Center (HSOAC), a federally funded research and development center operated by RAND on behalf of the Department of Homeland Security, has developed a contingency planning how-to guide, a planning template, and an accompanying introductory guide for decisionmakers to support planning efforts that can further these discussions.[8]

Areas for Further Research

We have noted several times that the field of cyber incident response that crosses multiple organizations and affects potentially multiple sectors is emerging, and one in which the United States has little experience in planning for and executing response. Our recommendations above are intended to further planning and learning among stakeholders to prepare better for future response. In addition to these practical steps, we conclude that there are additional areas requiring further research, to which we now turn.

8 Kotila et al., forthcoming.

Research on Governance Mechanisms and Their Improvement

In this report, we have provided an initial exploration into the response mechanisms for different forms of incidents. We have noted that there are differences in phases, decision points, and the nature of impacts across incident types and the stakeholders involved in that response. To improve incident management, there is a need for continued empirical work focused on the governance structures for different significant events. This work would delve deeper into addressing who the incident responders are, the types of capabilities they bring to bear, and how those responders integrate those capabilities currently in response. Further research into how these stakeholders coordinate their efforts currently and collaborate to determine, based on real-world experience and exercises, what forms of collaboration are most effective and where coordination can break down would vastly improve planning and execution of response. Additionally, this research could address whether top-down processes or more federated responses are more effective and why.

Principles for High-Reliability Networked Response

All of the hazard contexts we reviewed revealed that effective response to a significant incident is a multistakeholder endeavor, involving collaboration across government agencies and different sectors of society, including NGOs and individuals. In some cases, this networked response appears to operate effectively in extreme conditions, creating a reliable response even when the structures, processes, and individual responders may not be fully prepared to respond. However, there are also many examples of failure in which effective response foundered because of unreliable, incomplete, or unprepared response infrastructure, processes, or organizations. Previous research on operating reliably under extreme conditions has focused primarily on the organization as unit of analysis, not networked reliability. More research is needed to focus on the network, identifying the conditions that can be put in place to ensure response networked reliability. This would provide Department of Homeland Security and other incident responders a path forward for targeting investments to ensure response to significant incidents.

Abbreviations

CBRN	chemical, biological, radiological, or nuclear
CISA	Cybersecurity and Infrastructure Security Agency
COVID-19	coronavirus disease 2019
EOC	emergency operations center
ESF	Emergency Support Function
FBI	Federal Bureau of Investigation
FEMA	Federal Emergency Management Agency
HSOAC	Homeland Security Operational Analysis Center
ICS NIMS	Incident Command System and National Incident Management System
IT	information technology
NCF	National Critical Function
NCIRP	National Cyber Incident Response Plan
NGO	non-governmental organization
ODNI	Office of the Director of National Intelligence
PHEP	public health emergency preparedness
PPD	Presidential Policy Directive
SLTT	state, local, territorial, and tribal
UCG	Unified Coordination Group

References

28 C.F.R. Section 0.85—*See* Code of Federal Regulations Title 28, Chapter I, Department of Justice, Part 0, Organization of the Department of Justice, Subpart B, Federal Bureau of Investigation, Section 0.85, General Functions.

Altman, Drew, "Understanding the U.S. Failure on Coronavirus—An Essay by Drew Altman," *BMJ*, Vol. 370, No. 3417, September 2020.

Barnett, Daniel J., George S. Everly Jr., Cindy L. Parker, and Jonathan M. Links, "Applying Educational Gaming to Public Health Workforce Emergency Preparedness," *American Journal of Preventive Medicine*, Vol. 28, No. 4, 2005, pp. 390–395.

Bartock, Michael, Jeffrey Cichonski, Murugiah Souppaya, Matthew Smith, Gregory Witte, and Karen Scarfone, *Guide for Cybersecurity Event Recovery*, Gaithersburg, Md.: National Institute of Standards and Technology, SP 800-184, December 2016.

Bernton, Hal, Mike Carter, David Heath, and James Neff, "The Terrorist Within: The Story Behind One Man's Holy War Against America," *Seattle Times*, June 23–July 7, 2002.

Bhattacharjees, Yudhijit, "The Curse of the White Powder," *Slate*, January 30, 2012.

Bosher, Lee, Ksenia Chmutina, and Dewald van Niekerk, "Stop Going Around in Circles: Towards a Reconceptualisation of Disaster Risk Management Phases," *Disaster Prevention and Management: An International Journal*, Vol. 30, No. 4/5, April 2021, pp. 525–537.

California Office of Emergency Services, "My Hazards," webpage, undated. As of September 14, 2021:
https://myhazards.caloes.ca.gov

Centers for Disease Control and Prevention, "COVID-19," webpage, undated. As of September 14, 2021:
https://www.cdc.gov/coronavirus/2019-ncov/index.html

Centers for Medicare and Medicaid Services, "Ongoing Emergencies & Disasters," webpage, last modified December 1, 2021. As of January 26, 2022:
https://www.cms.gov/About-CMS/Agency-Information/Emergency/EPRO/Current-Emergencies/Ongoing-emergencies

Central Office for Recovery, Reconstruction and Resiliency, *Transformation and Innovation in the Wake of Devastation: An Economic and Disaster Recovery Plan for Puerto Rico*, August 8, 2018. As of October 18, 2021:
https://recovery.pr/documents/pr-transformation-innovation-plan-congressional-submission-080818.pdf

Chamberlin, Margaret, Adeyemi Theophilus Okunogbe, Melinda Moore, and Mahshid Abir, *Intra-Action Report—A Dynamic Tool for Emergency Managers and Policymakers: A Proof of Concept and Illustrative Application to the 2014–2015 Ebola Crisis*, Santa Monica, Calif.: RAND Corporation, PE-147-RC, 2015. As of October 18, 2021:
https://www.rand.org/pubs/perspectives/PE147.html

Chandra, Anita, Meagan Cahill, Douglas Yeung, and Rachel Ross, *Toward an Initial Conceptual Framework to Assess Community Allostatic Load: Early Themes from Literature Review and Community Analyses on the Role of Cumulative Community Stress*, Santa Monica, Calif.: RAND Corporation, RR-2559-RWJ, 2018. As of July 13, 2021:
https://www.rand.org/pubs/research_reports/RR2559.html

CISA—*See* Cybersecurity and Infrastructure Security Agency.

Clark-Ginsberg, Aaron, and Elizabeth L. Petrun Sayers, "Communication Missteps During COVID-19 Hurt Those Already Most at Risk," *Journal of Contingencies and Crisis Management*, Vol. 28, No. 4, June 2020, pp. 482–484.

Code of Federal Regulations Title 28, Chapter I, Department of Justice, Part 0, Organization of the Department of Justice, Subpart B, Federal Bureau of Investigation, Section 0.85, General Functions. As of March 17, 2022:
https://www.ecfr.gov/current/title-28/chapter-I/part-0/subpart-P/section-0.85

Collier, Stephen, and Andrew Lakoff, "The Vulnerability of Vital Systems: How 'Critical Infrastructure' Became a Security Problem," in Myriam Dunn and Kristian S. Kristensen, eds., *The Politics of Securing the Homeland: Critical Infrastructure, Risk and Securitisation*, London: Routledge, 2008, pp. 40–62.

Commonwealth of Massachusetts, "Office of Preparedness and Emergency Management," website, undated. As of February 28, 2022:
https://www.mass.gov/orgs/
office-of-preparedness-and-emergency-management

Computer Security Resource Center, "Mitigate," webpage, undated. As of March 17, 2022:
https://csrc.nist.gov/glossary/term/mitigate

Criswell, Deanne, "FEMA Administrator Deanne Criswell's Remarks to the 2021 IAEM Conference," webpage, October 18, 2021. As of October 26, 2021:
https://www.fema.gov/fact-sheet/
fema-administrator-deanne-criswells-remarks-2021-iaem-conference

Crowdstrike, *2021 Global Threat Report*, Sunnyvale, Calif., 2021. As of January 24, 2022:
https://www.crowdstrike.com/resources/reports/global-threat-report-2021/

Cybersecurity and Infrastructure Security Agency, "CISA National Cyber Incident Scoring System," webpage, undated-a. As of October 30, 2021:
https://us-cert.cisa.gov/CISA-National-Cyber-Incident-Scoring-System

Cybersecurity and Infrastructure Security Agency, "Cyber Storm: Securing Cyber Space," webpage, undated-b. As of October 26, 2021:
https://www.cisa.gov/cyber-storm-securing-cyber-space

Cybersecurity and Infrastructure Security Agency, "National Critical Functions," webpage, undated-c. As of March 29, 2021:
https://www.cisa.gov/national-critical-functions

Cybersecurity and Infrastructure Security Agency, "CISA Launches New Joint Cyber Defense Collaborative," webpage, August 5, 2021. As of August 23, 2021:
https://www.cisa.gov/news/2021/08/05/cisa-launches-new-joint-cyber-defense-collaborative

Department of Defense, Office of Inspector General, *Audit of the Department of Defense's Implementation of the Memorandums Between the Department of Defense and the Department of Homeland Security Regarding Cybersecurity and Cyberspace Operations*, Washington, D.C., DODIG-2021-100, July 13, 2021.

Department of Health and Human Services, "Public Health Emergency Declarations," webpage, last updated March 14, 2022. As of March 17, 2022:
https://www.phe.gov/emergency/news/healthactions/phe/Pages/default.aspx

Department of Homeland Security, "National Terrorism Advisory System," webpage, undated-a. As of March 17, 2022:
https://www.dhs.gov/national-terrorism-advisory-system

Department of Homeland Security, "Resource Typing Library Tool," online catalogue, version 1.6.11, undated-b. As of March 17, 2022:
https://rtlt.preptoolkit.fema.gov/Public

Department of Homeland Security, *National Cyber Incident Response Plan*, Washington, D.C., December 2016.

Department of Homeland Security, *Planning Considerations: Complex Coordinated Terrorist Attacks*, Washington, D.C., July 2018.

Department of Homeland Security, *Strategic Framework for Countering Terrorism and Targeted Violence*, Washington, D.C., September 2019.

Department of Homeland Security, "DHS/CISA/PIA–020 Private Sector Clearance Program for Critical Infrastructure," webpage, last updated November 12, 2021. As of March 17, 2022:
https://www.dhs.gov/publication/dhs-nppd-pia-020a-private-sector-clearance-program-critical-infrastructure

Department of Justice and the Federal Bureau of Investigation, *National Response Plan: Terrorism Incident Law Enforcement and Investigation Annex*, Washington, D.C., December 2004. As of October 25, 2021: https://www.fema.gov/sites/default/files/2020-07/fema_incident-annex_terrorism-law-enforcement.pdf

Directive-Type Memorandum 17-007, "Interim Policy and Guidance for Defense Support to Cyber Incident Response," U.S. Department of Defense, June 21, 2017. As of October 13, 2021: https://www.esd.whs.mil/DD/DoD-Issuances/DTM/

Domínguez, Daniela G., Dellanira García, David A. Martínez, and Belinda Hernandez-Arriaga, "Leveraging the Power of Mutual Aid, Coalitions, Leadership, and Advocacy During COVID-19," *American Psychologist*, Vol. 75, No. 7, October 2020, pp. 909–918.

Drabek, Thomas E., and David A. McEntire, "Emergent Phenomena and the Sociology of Disaster: Lessons, Trends and Opportunities from the Research Literature," *Disaster Prevention and Management: An International Journal*, Vol. 12, No. 2, 2003.

Dragos, Inc., *CRASHOVERRIDE: Analysis of the Threat to Electric Grid Operations*, Washington, D.C., June 2017.

Dragos, Inc., *Industrial Control System Threats*, Hanover, Md., March 1, 2018.

Dragos, Inc., *ICS Cybersecurity Year in Review 2020*, Washington, D.C., 2021. As of January 24, 2022: https://www.dragos.com/year-in-review/#section-report.

Ellis, Ryan, *Letters, Power Lines, and Other Dangerous Things: The Politics of Infrastructure Security*, Cambridge, Mass.: MIT Press, 2020.

Eversley, Melanie, "12 Years After, WTC Debris Still Sifted for Remains," *USA Today*, April 6, 2013. As of February 12, 2022: https://www.usatoday.com/story/news/nation/2013/04/06/world-trade-center-debris/2058763/

Federal Bureau of Investigation, "Famous Cases and Criminals: Amerithrax or Anthrax Investigation," webpage, undated-a. As of October 25, 2021: https://www.fbi.gov/history/famous-cases/amerithrax-or-anthrax-investigation

Federal Bureau of Investigation, "Terrorism 2002–2005," webpage, undated-b. As of August 23, 2021: https://www.fbi.gov/stats-services/publications/terrorism-2002-2005

Federal Bureau of Investigation, "What Is the FBI's Role in Combating Terrorism?" webpage, undated-c. As of October 26, 2021: https://www.fbi.gov/about/faqs/what-is-the-fbis-role-in-combating-terrorism

Federal Bureau of Investigation, Internet Crime Complaint Center, *Internet Crime Report 2020*, Washington, D.C., 2020.

FEMA—*See* Federal Emergency Management Agency.

Federal Emergency Management Agency, "National Risk Index," webpage, undated-a. As of September 14, 2021:
https://hazards.fema.gov/nri/map

Federal Emergency Management Agency, "Pub 1 and Core Values," webpage, undated-b. As of October 18, 2021:
https://www.fema.gov/about/pub-1

Federal Emergency Management Agency, *Managing the Emergency Consequences of Terrorist Incidents: Interim Planning Guide for State and Local Governments*, Washington, D.C., July 2002. As of October 25, 2021:
https://www.fema.gov/pdf/plan/managingemerconseq.pdf

Federal Emergency Management Agency, *National Preparedness Goal*, Washington, D.C., September 2015. As of January 31, 2021:
https://www.fema.gov/sites/default/files/2020-06/national_preparedness_goal_2nd_edition.pdf

Federal Emergency Management Agency, "Emergency Support Function #8–Public Health and Medical Services Annex," June 2016.

Federal Emergency Management Agency, *National Incident Management System, Third Edition*, Washington, D.C., October 2017.

Federal Emergency Management Agency, *Are You Ready? An In-Depth Guide to Citizen Preparedness*, Washington, D.C., P-2064, September 2020a.

Federal Emergency Management Agency, "National Level Exercise," webpage, updated July 21, 2020b. As of October 26, 2021:
https://www.fema.gov/emergency-managers/national-preparedness/exercises/national-level-exercise

Federal Emergency Management Agency, "National Level Exercise 2020," website, updated July 23, 2020c. As of February 13, 2022:
https://www.fema.gov/emergency-managers/planning-exercises/nle/2020

Federal Emergency Management Agency, "Whole Community," webpage, updated October 6, 2020d. As of March 17, 2020:
https://www.fema.gov/glossary/whole-community

Federal Emergency Management Agency, "National Response Framework," webpage, last updated October 15, 2021. As of March 16, 2022:
https://www.fema.gov/emergency-managers/national-preparedness/frameworks/response

Federal Emergency Management Agency, "Historic Disasters," webpage, last updated January 4, 2022. As of March 16, 2022: https://www.fema.gov/disaster/historic

Financial Stability Board, *Effective Practices for Cyber Incident Response and Recovery: Final Report*, Basel, Switzerland, October 19, 2020.

Financial Stability Board, "Cyber Resilience," webpage, last updated January 6, 2021. As of March 17, 2022: https://www.fsb.org/work-of-the-fsb/financial-innovation-and-structural-change/cyber-resilience/

Frontline, "Other Millennium Attacks," webpage, undated. As of September 14, 2021: https://www.pbs.org/wgbh/pages/frontline/shows/trail/inside/attacks.html

Garfinkel, Simson, "Anti-Forensics: Techniques, Detection and Countermeasures," 2nd International Conference on i-Warfare and Security, Monterey, Calif.: March 8–9, 2007.

Gerencser, Mark, Alex Gorsky, and Jeh C. Johnson, *Findings and Recommendations of the BENS Commission on the National Response Enterprise: A Call to Action*, Washington, D.C.: Business Executives for National Security, February 2021.

Greenberg, Andy, "The Untold Story of NotPetya, the Most Devastating Cyberattack in History," *Wired*, August 22, 2018. As of March 17, 2022: https://www.wired.com/story/notpetya-cyberattack-ukraine-russia-code-crashed-the-world/

Greenberg, Andy, *Sandworm: A New Era of Cyberwar and the Hunt for the Kremlin's Most Dangerous Hackers*, New York: Anchor Books, 2020.

Halpern, Lucy Wang, "The Politicization of COVID-19," *AJN The American Journal of Nursing*, Vol. 120, No. 11, November 2020, pp. 19–20.

Henriquez, Maria, "Hacker Breaks into Florida Water Treatment Facility, Changes Chemical Levels," *Security*, February 9, 2021.

Idaho National Laboratory, "Consequence-Driven Cyber-Informed Engineering," webpage, undated. As of October 26, 2021: https://inl.gov/cce/

International Association of Emergency Managers, "History of IAEM," webpage, undated. As of October 18, 2021: https://www.iaem.org/History-of-IAEM

International Federation of Red Cross and Red Crescent Societies, *Early Warning, Early Action: Mechanisms for Rapid Decision-Making*, Geneva, Switzerland, July 2014.

Ives, Mike, "California's Fires Are Stretching Crews and Stranding Evacuees," *New York Times*, August 20, 2021.

Jackson, Brian A., D. J. Peterson, James T. Bartis, Tom LaTourrette, Irene T. Brahmakulam, Ari Houser, and Jerry M. Sollinger, *Protecting Emergency Responders: Lessons Learned from Terrorist Attacks*, Santa Monica, Calif.: RAND Corporation, CF-176-OSTP, 2002. As of March 13, 2022: https://www.rand.org/pubs/conf_proceedings/CF176.html

"JBS: Cyber-Attack Hits World's Largest Meat Supplier," *BBC News*, June 2, 2021.

Jenkins, Brian Michael, "New Age of Terrorism," in David Kamien, ed., *McGraw-Hill Homeland Security Handbook*, New York: McGraw Hill, 2006, pp. 117–130.

Kaplan, Fred, *Dark Territory: The Secret History of Cyber War*, New York: Simon & Schuster, 2016a.

Kaplan, Fred, "'WarGames' and Cybersecurity's Debt to a Hollywood Hack," *New York Times*, February 19, 2016b.

Kario, Kazuomi, Bruce S. McEwen, and Thomas G. Pickering, "Disasters and the Heart: A Review of the Effects of Earthquake-Induced Stress on Cardiovascular Disease," *Hypertension Research*, Vol. 26, No 5, 2003, pp. 355–367.

Kelman, Ilan, *Disaster by Choice: How Our Actions Turn Natural Hazards into Catastrophes*, Oxford, United Kingdom: Oxford University Press, 2020.

King, Angus, and Mike Gallagher, *Cyberspace Solarium Commission: Final Report*, Arlington, Va., March 2020.

Kishore, Nishant, Domingo Marqués, Ayesha Mahmud, Mathew V. Kiang, Irmary Rodriguez, Arlan Fuller, Peggy Ebner, Cecilia Sorensen, Fabio Racy, Jay Lemery, Leslie Maas, Jennifer Leaning, Rafael A. Irizarry, Satchit Balsari, and Caroline O. Buckee, "Mortality in Puerto Rico after Hurricane Maria," *New England Journal of Medicine*, Vol. 379, No. 2, 2018, pp. 162–170.

Knowles, Scott Gabriel, *The Disaster Experts: Mastering Risk in Modern America*, Philadelphia: University of Pennsylvania Press, 2012.

Kotila, Brodi, Quentin E. Hodgson, Benjamin Boudreaux, Ian Mitch, Aaron Clark-Ginsberg, Sale Lilly, Kristin J. Leuschner, Tom Wingfield, *Planning for Significant Cyber Incidents: An Introduction for Decisionmakers*, Homeland Security Operational Analysis Center operated by the RAND Corporation, RR-A1265-1, forthcoming.

Lakoff, Andrew, *Unprepared: Global Health in a Time of Emergency*, Oakland, Calif.: University of California Press, 2017.

Lewis, Matthew W., Edward W. Chan, Christopher Nelson, Andrew Hackbarth, Christine Anne Vaughan, Alonzo L. Plough, and Brit K. Oiulfstad, "Wearing Many Hats: Lessons About Preparedness and Routine Public Health from the H1n1 Response," in M. Stoto and M Higdon, eds., *The Public Health Response to 2009 H1N1: A Systems Perspective*, Oxford, United Kingdom: Oxford University Press, 2015.

Lindell, Michael K., "Disaster Studies," *Current Sociology*, Vol. 61, No. 5–6, 2013, pp. 797–825.

Lindsay, Bruce R., *Stafford Act Assistance and Acts of Terrorism*, Washington, D.C.: Congressional Research Service, R44801, last updated January 16, 2019.

Maani, Nason, and Sandro Galea, "COVID-19 and Underinvestment in the Public Health Infrastructure of the United States," *Milbank Quarterly*, Vol. 98, No. 2, June 2020.

Maxwell, Daniel G., and Peter Walker, *Shaping the Humanitarian World*, London: Routledge, 2014.

Meyer, Josh, "Border Arrest Stirs Fear of Terrorist Cells in U.S.," *Los Angeles Times*, March 11, 2001.

Miller, Maggie, "White House 'Standing Down' Emergency Response Groups to SolarWinds, Microsoft Hacks," *The Hill*, April 19, 2021.

MITRE ATT&CK, homepage, undated. As of April 12, 2022: https://attack.mitre.org/

National Academies of Sciences, Engineering and Medicine, *Strengthening the Disaster Resilience of the Academic Biomedical Research Community: Protecting the Nation's Investment*, Washington, D.C.: National Academies Press, 2017.

National Cyber Security Centre, *NCSC Annual Review 2021*, London, November 17, 2021.

National Hurricane Program, "Hurrevac," webpage, undated. As of September 14, 2021:
http://www.hurrevac.com/

National Infrastructure Advisory Council, *Actionable Cyber Intelligence: An Executive-Led Collaborative Model*, Washington, D.C., December 2020.

National Oceanic and Atmospheric Administration, "Billion-Dollar Weather and Climate Disasters: Overview," webpage, undated. As of March 16, 2022: https://www.ncdc.noaa.gov/billions/

National Severe Storms Laboratory, "Severe Weather 101—Floods," webpage, undated. As of September 14, 2021:
https://www.nssl.noaa.gov/education/svrwx101/floods/

Nelson, Christopher, Nicole Lurie, Jeffrey Wasserman, and Sarah Zakowski, "Conceptualizing and Defining Public Health Emergency Preparedness," *American Journal of Public Health*, Vol. 97, Suppl. 1, 2007, pp. S9–S11.

Newman, Lily Hay, "How an Accidental 'Kill Switch' Slowed Friday's Massive Ransomware Attack," *Wired*, May 13, 2017.

Nomura, Shuhei, Alexander J. Q. Parsons, Mayo Hirabayashi, Ryo Kinoshita, Yi Liao, and Susan Hodgson, "Social Determinants of Mid-to Long-Term Disaster Impacts on Health: A Systematic Review," *International Journal of Disaster Risk Reduction*, Vol. 16 , 2016, pp. 53–67.

North American Electric Reliability Corporation, "GridEx," webpage, undated. As of October 26, 2021:
https://www.nerc.com/pa/CI/ESISAC/Pages/GridEx.aspx

NATO Cooperative Cyber Defence Centre of Excellence, "NotPetya and WannaCry Call for a Joint Response from International Community," webpage, undated. As of March 17, 2022:
https://ccdcoe.org/news/2017/notpetya-and-wannacry-call-for-a-joint-response-from-international-community/

ODNI—*See* Office of the Director of National Intelligence.

Office of the Director of National Intelligence, "Cyber Threat Framework," webpage, undated-a. As of March 17, 2022:
https://www.dni.gov/index.php/cyber-threat-framework

Office of the Director of National Intelligence, "Cyber Threat Intelligence Integration Center," webpage, undated-b. As of April 22, 2022:
https://www.dni.gov/index.php/241-about/organization/cyber-threat-intelligence-integration-center

Public Law 116-283, William M. (Mac) Thornberry National Defense Authorization Act for Fiscal Year 2021, January 1, 2021.

Quarantelli, E. L., "The Early History of the Disaster Research Center," white paper, University of Delaware, undated. As of October 18, 2021:
https://www.drc.udel.edu/content-sub-site/Documents/DRC%20Early%20History.pdf

RAND Corporation, "Hurricanes Irma and Maria: Impact and Aftermath," webpage, undated. As of October 13, 2021:
https://www.rand.org/hsrd/hsoac/projects/puerto-rico-recovery/hurricanes-irma-and-maria.html

Red Cross, "Common Disasters Across the U.S.," webpage, undated. As of August 23, 2021:
https://www.redcross.org/get-help/how-to-prepare-for-emergencies/common-natural-disasters-across-us.html#all

Reed, Jonathan, "U.S. Congress Approves Strengthening American Cybersecurity Act," *Security Intelligence*, March 30, 2022. As of April 28, 2022: https://securityintelligence.com/news/us-congress-approves-american-cybersecurity-act/

Rinaldi, Steven M., James P. Peerenboom, and Terrence K. Kelly, "Identifying, Understanding, and Analyzing Critical Infrastructure Interdependences," *IEEE Control Systems Magazine*, December 2001, pp. 11–25.

Roberts, Patrick S., *Disasters and the American State: How Politicians, Bureaucrats, and the Public Prepare for the Unexpected*, Cambridge, United Kingdom: Cambridge University Press, 2013.

Rose, D. A., S. Murthy, J. Brooks, and J. Bryant, "The Evolution of Public Health Emergency Management as a Field of Practice," *American Journal of Public Health*, Vol. 107, No. S2, September 2017, pp. S126–S33.

Sandia National Laboratory, "IDART: Information Design Assurance Red Team," webpage, undated. As of October 26, 2021: https://casa.sandia.gov/idart/

SANS and Electricity Information Sharing and Analysis Center, *Analysis of the Cyber Attack on the Ukrainian Power Grid: Defense Use Case*, Washington, D.C., March 18, 2016.

Seeger, Matthew W., Laura E. Pechta, Simani M. Price, Keri M. Lubell, Dale A. Rose, Saloni Sapru, Melanie C. Chansky, and Belinda J. Smith, "A Conceptual Model for Evaluating Emergency Risk Communication in Public Health," *Health Security*, Vol. 16, No. 3, 2018, pp. 193–203.

Sirleaf, Ellen Johnson, and Helen Clark, "Report of the Independent Panel for Pandemic Preparedness and Response: Making COVID-19 the Last Pandemic," *The Lancet*, Vol. 398, No. 10295, July 10, 2021, pp. P101–P103.

Stambler, Kimberly S., and Joseph A. Barbera, "The Evolution of Shortcomings in Incident Command System: Revisions Have Allowed Critical Management Functions to Atrophy," *Journal of Emergency Management*, Weston, Mass., Vol. 13, No. 6, 2015, pp. 509–518.

Stockton, Paul N., *Superstorm Sandy: Implications for Designing a Post–Cyber Attack Power Restoration System*, Laurel, Md.: Johns Hopkins University Applied Physics Laboratory, March 31, 2016.

"Timeline: How the Anthrax Terror Unfolded," National Public Radio, February 15, 2011. As of October 25, 2021: https://www.npr.org/2011/02/15/93170200/timeline-how-the-anthrax-terror-unfolded

Trust for America's Health, *The Impact of Chronic Underfunding on America's Public Health System: Trends, Risks, and Recommendations, 2020*, Washington, D.C.: April 2020.

"Tube Log Shows Initial Confusion," *BBC News*, July 12, 2005.

Turton, William, and Kartikay Mehrotra, "Hackers Breached Colonial Pipeline Using Compromised Password," *Bloomberg*, June 4, 2021.

Twigg, John, and Irina Mosel, "Emergent Groups and Spontaneous Volunteers in Urban Disaster Response," *Environment and Urbanization*, Vol. 29, No. 2, 2017, pp. 443–458.

U.S. Code Title 18, Section 2331, Definitions, amended as of October 3, 2018.

U.S. Geological Survey, "Early Warning," webpage, undated-a. As of April 11, 2022:
https://www.usgs.gov/programs/earthquake-hazards/science/early-warning

U.S. Geological Survey, "Frequently Asked Questions: How Can Climate Change Affect Natural Disasters?" webpage, undated-b. As of October 30, 2021:
https://www.usgs.gov/faqs/how-can-climate-change-affect-natural-disasters-1?qt-news_science_products=0#qt-news_science_products

U.S. Geological Survey, "Frequently Asked Questions: Why Do Earthquakes in Other Countries Seem to Cause More Damage and Casualties Than Earthquakes in the U.S.?" webpage, undated-c. As of September 14, 2021:
https://www.usgs.gov/faqs/why-do-earthquakes-other-countries-seem-cause-more-damage-and-casualties-earthquakes-us?qt-news_science_products=0#qt-news_science_products

U.S. House of Representatives, Select Bipartisan Committee to Investigate the Preparation for, and Response to Hurricane Katrina, *A Failure of Initiative: Final Report of the Select Bipartisan Committee to Investigate the Preparation for and Response to Hurricane Katrina*, Report 109-377, Washington, D.C.: U.S. Government Printing Office, February 15, 2006.

White House, Office of the Press Secretary, "Presidential Policy Directive–United States Cyber Incident Coordination," presidential memorandum, July 26, 2016. As of August 23, 2021:
https://obamawhitehouse.archives.gov/the-press-office/2016/07/26/presidential-policy-directive-united-states-cyber-incident

Wisner, Ben, Piers Blaikie, Terry Cannon, and Ian Davis, *At Risk: Natural Hazards, People's Vulnerability and Disasters*, London: Routledge, 2004.

World Economic Forum, "Securing a Common Future in Cyberspace," video, January 24, 2018. As of October 13, 2021:
https://youtu.be/Tqe3K3D7TnI